WE Summit Together

2020

A Collection of Empowering Stories

By Empowered Women

First Published in 2020 by
Success in Doing Publications

www.wesummit.ie

ISBN: 978-1-9160176-1-0

Contents

Introduction
by Donna Kennedy

Imagine you have a battery-operated torch. You want to light it up, so you flick the on-switch. Nothing happens. You try again. Still nothing. You shake it, as if by some miracle that will switch it on. Still nothing. Then, after a bit of bewilderment and frustration, you realise that there are no batteries in it. Of course, without battery power, it would be crazy to think it would work; it's just a bunch of plastic and metal matter after all, right? Sure, a torch has the *potential* to function and shine, but without battery power nothing happens. So, using your common sense, you get some batteries, pop them in and then hit the on-switch. Hey presto, the torch is powered up, it shines and you're happy!

Now you may be wondering why I am talking about a torch and batteries, when this book is meant to be about empowerment? Well, before we get into reading the chapters to follow, I want you to see just how much potential you have (you have more than you think!) because once you understand it, your approach to reading the rest of the book might be quite different.

Liken that torch to you and your potential. You (your mind and body) are made of cells (lots of them) but if those cells are left unstimulated, i.e. the power button isn't switched on, the cells are nothing more than matter, just like a torch without batteries. However, when cells are given energy or electrical charge, like a torch is energised, it's a different ball game altogether. With electrical stimulation electrical impulses shoot back and forth between our cells, lighting up a whole sensory communication network within us. And when those cells act collectively, our potential is huge! The key is to know how to switch on the power button.

Electrical impulses are responsible for our very life, how we think, see, hear, move, feel etc. In fact, we now have research to show that even at conception a stunning explosion of zinc "fireworks" occurs when a human egg is activated by a sperm enzyme, and the size of these "sparks" of electricity is a direct measure of the quality of the egg and its ability to develop into an embryo, i.e. you, a living human being. Where the source of that electricity comes from is anyone's guess, but one thing we know for certain is that it is there, we conduct it, and if we are open minded enough to embrace it, we can use it get results. To ignore the importance of that energy would be naïve at best. Energy and how we use it is the foundation of all we do. It is our power source. Empowerment is defined as *given power*.

Now I'm not talking about daisy chain notions here, what I am about to share with you is studied and supported in science. And thankfully, due to advanced technology, you don't need to be a genius to appreciate how it works. Today, in a laboratory, we can see, measure and monitor that power by observing electromagnetic fields, frequency, vibration and potential, but most importantly, we now know how to use the energy to get results, including results in our personal lives.

Did you know that every cell in your body has electrical energy, with a charge and potential of about 1.4 volts? The voltage of an AA battery is 1.5! Not only that, every cell has a negative voltage inside and positive voltage outside and, depending on your size, you have approximately 50 trillion "battery cells" in your body, which means you have approximately 70 trillion volts of electricity in your body right now! Can you imagine tapping into even a piece of that power? To put it into context you only need 240 volts to boil a kettle.

You see, you may just look like a bunch of matter, but you are not, you are a network of charged cells and subatomic particles, that continually communicate and interact with each other through electrical frequency waves. How those cells interact is determined by the rate of their vibration. Not only that, the energy even extends beyond your body and into your environment, responding and resonating with the people and things in it. For example. when you touch a door handle (or something else made of metal), an electrical charge imbalance occurs, and any excess of electrons jump from you to the knob. The tiny shock you feel is a result of the rapid movement of these electrons. So, although we can't always see the energy in motion, we can experience the results of it! Even it seems bizarre, we are in fact the same energy network. That said, doesn't it make sense to pay attention to the fact?

Once we thought the earth was flat. Now we know it's not. Can you imagine going back in time fifty years and telling people about your phone, a tiny gadget with the capacity to store thousands of songs, take pictures and videos, measure your heart rate and pulse, check the weather, watch movies, chat and talk with friends thousands of miles away while seeing their faces on a touch-screen — all wireless! You would be carted off to the nearest psychiatric hospital for assessment! And before the invention of the electron microscope, which made it possible to view objects as small as the diameter of an atom, nobody believed that something so small could even exist. But by embracing a new approach and using an electron beam instead of visible light, and an electron detector instead of our eyes, we can now see what's really going on. The key is to be open to new knowledge!

Research now shows us that we are electrically charged beings that interact with and respond to everything around us. We were born with a desire for continual development and expansion of our potential. We came into the world with sparkle, with a mindset of abundance and an excited curiosity to try new things. However, somewhere, somehow, that innate enthusiasm slowed down or possibly even stopped. So, what happened? Why did we go from feeling that we can do anything to doubting ourselves and our ability to reach our full potential? Why did we put limits on ourselves?

Well, when we are born, we are born into an environment of people. We are exposed to their frequency of vibration, their thoughts, beliefs and values, and it begins to mould us. We are given a *frame of knowledge* (not necessarily a good one) from which to base our lives on, 'This is true, this isn't', 'This is what we believe', 'This is what we don't believe', etc. and we innocently accept those programs, the same way you learned your language and developed your accent. If we are born into and continue to grow up in an environment with a high frequency of vibration, happy days. However, most people don't get that plain-sailing journey. In most cases, even if someone is born into a good environment, the frequency of vibration is disturbed at some point along the way, due to the people, experiences and challenges experienced in life. Of course, with little or no understanding of how to deal with this, and without being shown, it is easy to become overwhelmed and let life circumstance take *charge*. However, to be empowered we must take ownership of our lives and be *in charge, of* who we are and what we can become.

Are you prepared to think outside of what you already know, if it means becoming more empowered? Let's see! I'd like you to do the following exercise. Get a pen and *without picking your pen up off the paper*, I want you to connect all nine dots below using *four lines only*.

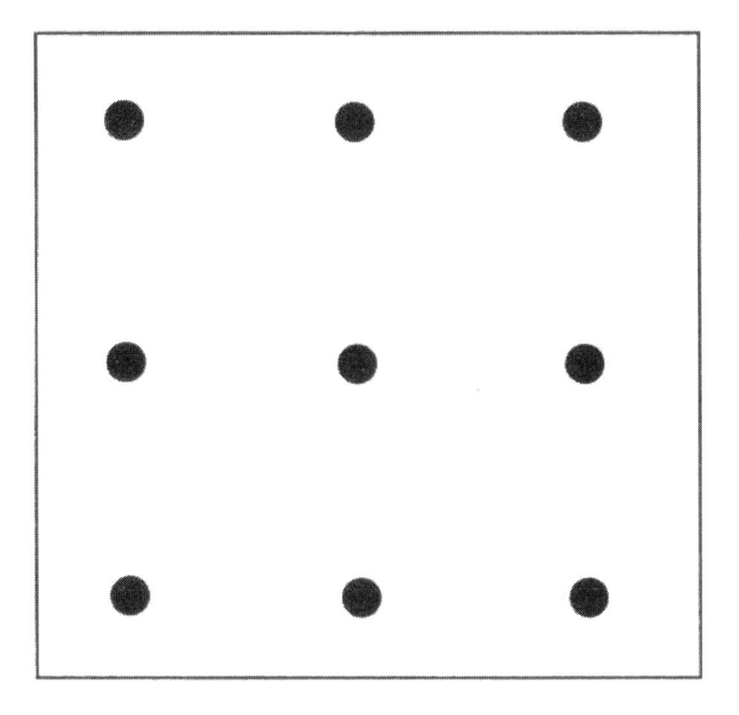

Tricky isn't it? Now let's see how it can be done by thinking in a different way.

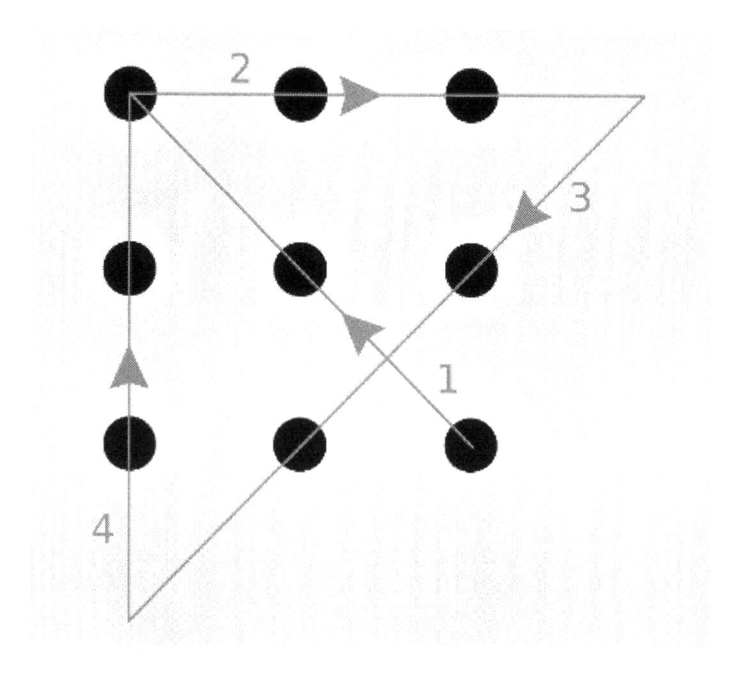

You see, if you are to become empowered, you need to think bigger. As such, I ask that as you read this book you become more open to new ways of looking at things. As you will see, it can be life transforming!

I was born into a loving environment. I was a happy little girl, full of sparkle and dreams, and I felt my potential was unlimited. Things were going along nicely (as they should) but then things changed. At seven years of age I was sexually assaulted. Somebody came to our home and basically took *charge* of me. They took my power. I didn't know how to deal with it, and unfortunately, because we don't come into life with a well-read survival guide, instead of getting help to deal with it, I shut down my emotions and spiralled into a drained existence. I recoiled into an emotionally confined "safety zone" in my mind. I started to starve myself, thinking it was a way to control my body again, and almost died in the process. I became entangled in **emotion** and I couldn't seem to move out of it.

In Latin **E** means *out of or out from*. Motion can be broken down into **mot**, which means to move, and the last part **ion**, is a charged atom. Emotion means to ***move energy out of*** something. Following the assault, I held the energy around it tight inside my mind, and I wasn't letting it move anywhere for anyone. I didn't want to feel it. But energy is not meant to be contained and cannot be contained without consequence. My consequence was that I developed anorexia and eventually fell into a short coma. It was a change-quickly-or-die scenario.

Thankfully, I eventually accepted help and with time I began to deal with what had happened. It wasn't easy, but I gradually let the emotions that I had attached to the assault move out and dissipate. I let them go. I had been living in a confined low frequency of vibration for a long time, and I had attached a lot of negative energy and negative habits to it. To change, I had to be open to change, to tap into a new frequency of vibration, so I could have a new conversation with life — a better one!

When I decided to commit to my recovery, it felt like I was hanging up the phone on someone nasty and choosing to make a phone call to someone nicer, in the hope that things would get better for me. I will use the analogy of a phone here to explain how I recovered, and how simply shifting our frequency can make or break us.

Make a Call

To call to someone on a phone you must first dial the number. As soon as you do, a frequency wave is immediately broadcast from your phone, bounces off an antenna and searches for the phone you are trying to call, amongst a huge network of frequencies. This process involves sending the frequency wave from your phone through a transmission box and as soon as it's processed, it quickly finds the phone you want to call, and you can have your conversation. Of course, your ability to connect the call in the first place will depend on four things:

1) Does your phone match the frequency of the phone you are trying to call? The phone will only resonate with a matching frequency.

2) Is it in range or are there obstacles that could block the transmission of the phone's frequency waves, such as buildings or enclosed confined spaces?

3) Are there things of different frequencies that could interfere with your signal?

4) Are there environmental factors such as storms that could interrupt your signal or cause the signal to drop?

Now let's liken the cell phone to you, your cells, the experiences you have and your life outcomes. Just like a cell phone, your "cells" have frequency. That frequency is broadcasted from you as a vibrating energy wave into your environment and goes on a search for a matching frequency. Like a phone filters the frequency wave through a transmission box, your brain filters through thoughts, beliefs and values, those you were given up to that point in your life. Once that part is complete, the frequency rapidly moves along in search of the people and experiences that match your frequency and resonates with them. For example, if you are in a low mood, you will find it easier to connect with people who are also in a low mood, but it's not going to be a very productive or enjoyable conversation. If you are fearful, you will find it easy to find things that scare you. If you don't respect yourself, people may be more inclined to disrespect you, and so on. Your "cell" will find people and things that resonate with you. Of course, this also depends on your ability to connect.

1) What range does your frequency have? Can you reach the people you want, or do you have to broaden your range?
2) Are there obstacles in your way? Have you confined yourself to small thinking or shut down your emotions? You must deal with obstacles, if you are to create space to connect with the people and things you want in your life. Had I not dealt with the obstacles that took up space in my mind, I would still be stuck and possibly dead.
3) Are there things interfering with your frequency that are causing your signal to drop? What are you allowing into your life? What or who are you listening to? What conversations are you having daily? Are they useful or productive? Choose empowering communication.
4) Environmental factors. Does your environment support your goals? If it doesn't, you might need to change it. Equip your mind with updated learnings so you can handle any unexpected "storms" that may arise. Life storms sometimes present unexpected experiences but it is up to you how you attach yourself to them. Be careful how much energy you attach to something. Energy flows where attention goes.

Pat Attention!

If you don't consciously pay attention to your life and how it is unfolding, you will run into problems. Have you ever met a person and later said, 'I didn't like the vibe I got from them' or 'They gave me a shiver up my spine' or 'I loved the buzz they created', yet you may not have known anything about them? You were picking up their frequency of vibration! But did you pay attention to it? To be empowered, you must consciously monitor the electrical field around you and all that is in it. Question things often, to make sure you stay connected to a high frequency of vibration; listen to your gut!

Remember when you were a kid, what was your favourite question? *Why,* of course! As children we question, question and question again. We are eager to continually explore and grow. But as time passes, we are told to *stop* asking why, so we eventually stop asking. 'That doesn't happen to people like us', 'That's only for the rich and famous', 'Isn't it well for some to be able to do that.' etc. To empower yourself, you must start questioning again. You must get your mind moving out of old patterns and thinking more freely, so you can move into a better frequency of vibration and explore your higher potential.

The Power of Frequency

Have a look at the following images. They represent a simple experiment to show the power of frequency and how impactful it can be in real life. In this experiment, a tone generator (below) was used to stimulate a neutral substance, sand in this case, to see if varying the levels of electrical frequency (measured in hertz or Hz for short) would affect the substance in different ways.

The sand was simply sprinkled on the metal plate but without energy flowing into the plate it just fell and settled.

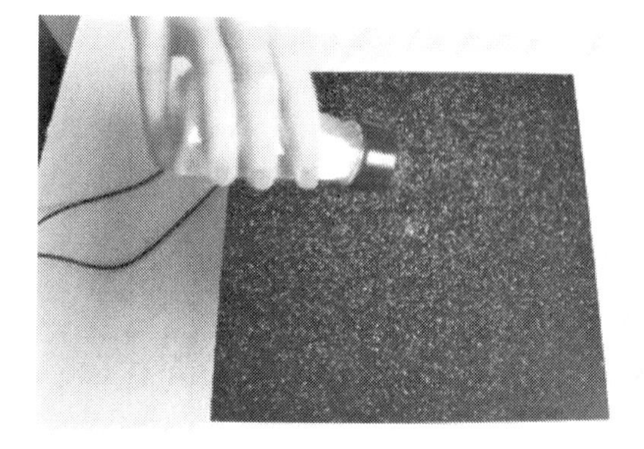

However, when the plate started to receive energy at various levels of frequency from the tone generator, the sand particles started to vibrate, and patterns started to emerge, depending on the frequency level being generated. As you will see the level of frequency made quite a difference!

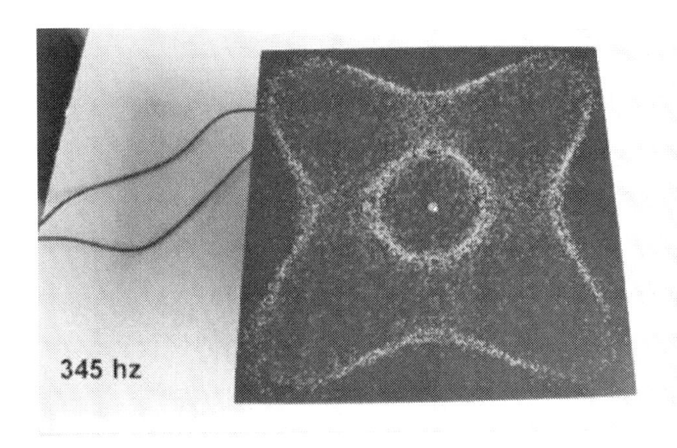
345 hz

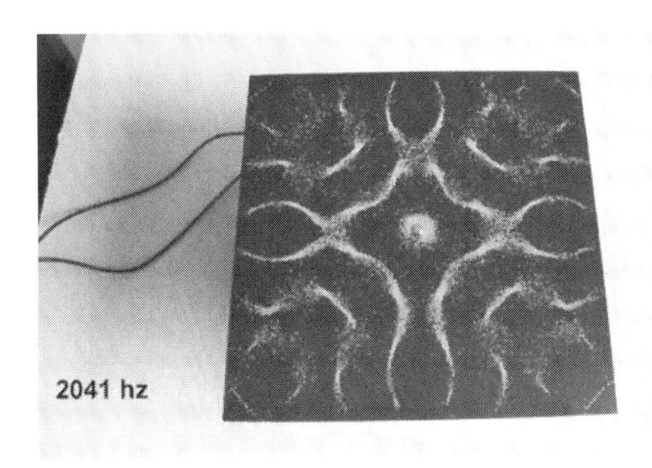
2041 hz

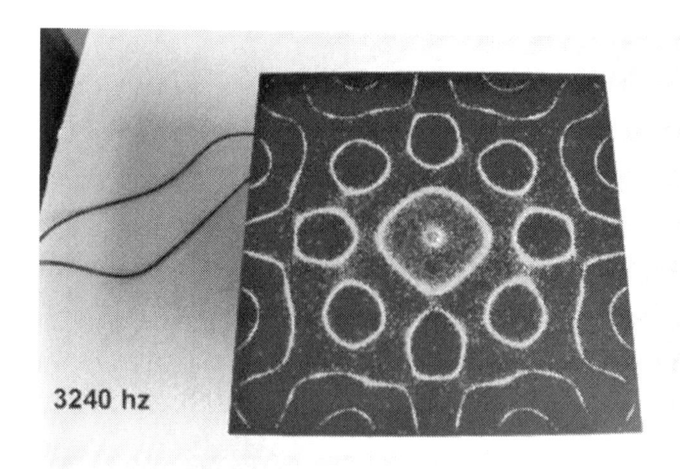

So, the question is, do you want to remain a neutral piece of matter in a limbo state that just settles wherever it's sprinkled, or do you want to a create an em-*power*-ed beautiful pattern in your life? It's up to you to choose the vibration of your life, but remember, the higher the frequency, the higher the vibration and the better your ability to create what you want. I personally chose to plug back into life because the alternative for me was death. Initially, I didn't know how, so I had to learn how the mind and body works and how we can, as human beings, put ourselves in an optimal vibration for better results. Then I implemented what I learned and here I am today — happy, confident and making great things happen.

Understanding Your Thoughts

During my research of the mind, I found many studies that have explored brain frequency to see if varying emotions have varying frequency levels based on how we think about experiences, and if they really affect our lives. Most of these studies used EEG (Electroencephalography) to record oscillations (magnitude of electric current or voltage) in different frequency ranges. Although clear EEG frequency correlates of specific emotions have so far not been conclusively shown, *patterns* of frequency distributions that distinguish different *representations of emotional experiences* have, i.e. frequency differs depending on whether we are thinking negatively or positively about our life experiences. Negative thoughts have a lower frequency than positive ones. To think negatively puts us in a weak state.

That said, if we want to increase our frequency of vibration for better life results, we need to make sure our thoughts and how we represent our life experiences in our mind are positive. If you're going around blaming the world and the people in it for your past, present of envisioned problems, it's not going to empower you. It will just put you into electrical chaos and keep you stuck. So, ask yourself how you can represent your life experiences differently. A classic example of this is when two people experience the same car crash. One person comes away from the experience with a disempowering representation, 'I could have died, but nobody would miss me anyway' and the other comes away from the experience with empowered thinking, 'I could have died. I'm committed to making every moment of my life joyous from now on.' Neither person enjoyed or deserved the car crash, but their representations of it determined how they felt and behaved afterwards. What representations of your life do you have? If they are not productive, you must view them differently. Instead of, for example, 'They hurt me and ruined my life', you could think, 'They hurt me, and I survived. I'm going to create the life I want as a stronger person.' It's all about how you represent experiences and the emotion to attach to them. Everything you think, say or feel changes your vibration, so choose wisely, if you want a more empowered life.

Letting Go

To get better life results, you must let go of any emotional baggage that is weighing you down. Blame and resentment are toxic, so if you are in the blaming zone, you most move out of it. Do you know who gets most hurt from feelings of anger, resentment, and hatred? You! It keeps you stuck. Letting go of things that hurt you is essential to a good vibration. You cannot be empowered if you hold onto pain or grudges. I'm not suggesting for one second that you pretend the experiences you had didn't exist, and I'm not asking you to excuse them, I am suggesting you don't allow the pain attached to your experiences drain you or affect you in a negative way. Release the thoughts and any negative emotion attached to them. Free them from the confines of your mind and body.

Gratitude

Looking for the good in your life isn't always easy, especially if there appears to be more bad than good. I used to see all the negative things in my life, so any beauty in it was clouded. But unless you can recognise what you *do have*, you cannot possibly expect any sort of abundance to come into your life. Did you know that what you have is someone else's dream? For example. you can read this, someone else can't. Let's be frank here, what do we all really have to complain about in the grand scheme of things? We are alive, and as long as we are, we have something to be grateful for. I'm sure you could list a hundred bad things in your life, if given time to list them, but will focusing on the negative allow you to receive the positive? Absolutely not. Remember, your cells look for matching frequency. If you want to be empowered, create positive energy around what you already have. Look at the simple things, for they are usually the most important and powerful. You will find that several of the authors here speak about the power of gratitude — it's powerful!

Kindness

There are so many empowering benefits from being kind to others. Studies have shown that witnessing and partaking in acts of kindness produces oxytocin (a hormone that aids in lowering blood pressure and inducing relaxation) and serotonin (a hormone responsible for good mood). In 2010 a Harvard Business School survey of happiness in 136 countries found that people who are altruistic, in this case people who gave charitable donations, were happiest. And according to research from Emory University, when you are kind to another person, your brain's pleasure and reward centres become highly active, as if you were the recipient of the good deed, a phenomenon called the "helper's high." It has even been shown that people who volunteer tend to experience fewer aches and pains and have a lower likelihood of dying early! Why? Your cells are at a much happier vibration and connect at high frequency!

The Importance of Your Team

Whose energetic field are you walking into? Tread carefully. Be around people who are good for you, people who help you feel good. Bring empowering people into your life; every person you meet interacts with and influences your electrical field.

Create a Why

It's important to have goals and aspirations. They don't have to be on the scale of climbing Mount Everest, but it's important you have something good to focus on. What positive thing would you do, if you didn't doubt yourself? What positive thing would you do, if you knew you would not fail? Play around with it, and once you find a focus, make sure you have a why. A why, a purpose or reason behind your goal, is the rocket fuel that will help you achieve it. Get as much energy around your goal as possible. Put a date on its achievement and announce it to people who might support you. The positive pressure will help you focus. List all the benefits of achieving the goal and all the negatives for not achieving it. Excite your cells into action!

Train your brain

In one of my books, *The Confidence to Succeed,* I speak about how our brain downloads information from the environment, like apps are downloaded onto a phone. You can only engage in an app, if it is downloaded and active on your phone, just as you can only engage in a program that is active in your mind. Every millisecond you are downloading information from your environment that is wiring your brain for automated responses and behaviours. You have undoubtedly downloaded some programmes that do not serve you or that have the potential to harm you, so sift through them and decide what ones who need to keep, let go of, update or newly install. It helps to get a pen and paper and write down the kind of programs you would need to have in your brain to be the best version of yourself. Then get to work on immersing your mind in the right information. In this book you will get the opportunity to do exercises that will help you do this.

Understand Optimal Cell Function.

Although we have a central intelligence, every one of our cells is an individual entity. Under a microscope a cell looks simple, but don't underestimate its power. When you look after your cells, your body and mind can function at their best and you can experience the result of it.

- Electrical conductivity.
  For our cells to communicate with one another, there needs to be a way of passing on the electrical impulses. We must remember we are 70% made of water. Fluids by themselves are not very good electric conductors, but the presence of salt and diverse ions in water turns the table, and this is why water is a very good electric conductor. Drink up!

- Nutrition

Cells form tissues - tissues form organs - organs form the human body, therefore less cells dying and more cells staying alive and healthy is empowering the human body to get to optimal health and energy by itself. Micronutrients are needed by every cell in the body. They either make things happen or they are needed by other nutrients to make things happen. They act as catalysts, transferring food into energy. Each individual mineral and trace element have specific functions in the body with magnesium taking part in over 300 reactions, for example. Make sure you have the vitamins, minerals, fatty acids, and amino acids that are required to keep the body functioning optimally. They keep your focus clear!

Develop Your Mind

Stretching and challenging your mind allows for the exploration of your potential. You were never meant to stop developing your mind, so *now* is your chance to change and grow. A more developed mind will increase your frequency of vibration in such a way that people of higher vibration can begin to connect and resonate with you, opening new conversations, new ideas, possibilities and opportunities for you. New learnings help you move more easily out of your old frame of knowledge, it broadens your range for potential growth.

In this book, you will have "conversations" through story with my team that can help you to move outside your old frame of thinking and into a more empowering space, so you can create the life you are truly capable of creating. This book is a tool for you to use to expand your thought processes, move emotion that doesn't serve you and help you reach places in your mind that you may have forgotten about. It may be a word, a sentence, an exercise or a whole perspective that resonates with you. And you may notice some commonalities within chapters — pay attention to them, there's a reason they are there! All I ask is that you take positive action on whatever resonates with you here, for nothing happens without action. It's time to stop settling, step up and raise your vibration. Now is your chance. Now is your time to shine!

Wake up!

by Kiera Ricci

Since our first gasp, our desperation for breath, here on this earth, we are developing, our minds, unconsciously building a picture of what the world means. The seeds of thought are moulding, shaping, warning, and creating our core beliefs moment to moment, but they are also distorting us.

At age twenty I was full of life, but I was also unconscious. I was aware of myself, but I wasn't sure if I was living. A life support device was forcing air to my lungs, I could just about feel the pumping of my heart, but all my power was focused on holding my soul tightly.

For what seemed like a lifetime, I had been tortured. I had been abused "quietly" and behind thick, tall, grand closed doors. Nobody knew, I was stuck in a living nightmare. A charming individual he was, loved by everyone but a perfect liar and manipulator. Who would have known, with such a perfect exterior?! Money and a glamorous lifestyle on the outside but violence behind closed doors. I endured physical, emotional and harsh psychological abuse. He made me think it was normal, I was the problem, it was my fault! It was my fault I broke my wrist, my fault I broke my arm, my fault I fell into the radiator, my fault I had a black eye and thick lip and couldn't be seen in public. He controlled every aspect of my life, even my life as a young entrepreneur had been stopped, eventually I wasn't even "allowed" to work. I was 5.5 stone in weight, and I was at my lowest in all aspects of my life. I plummeted from knowing a high experience of living life on my own terms, to being completely shattered. I had lost my spark. This unfortunate part of my life ended with a few months in intensive care and the possibility of not waking up.

*

I wondered if history was repeating itself because at 15-years-old I had escaped a similar nightmare. I was picked on by nasty childhood bullies since before I could remember. Kids can be awful! I was kicked in the stomach, kicked in the head, spat at, chewing gum was put in my hair, and I was followed home from the bus-stop, yet I was the quietest soul, I would never hurt anyone intentionally, so I wondered why were they intentionally killing me. I didn't want to be here, I wanted to disappear. I was totally lost, alone and being completely transparent, I wanted to end this life. I saw no way out.

But even at a young age, that fight-or-flight took me, removed me from that darkness, and I catapulted myself into a better life. Trying to remove myself from the bullies, I grew up quickly. I moved abroad, learned to speak Spanish, learned to drive, lived independently and started my first business accidentally. I tried to remove myself from the bullies so I could have a better life. I had bought a chihuahua as they were so beautiful and small enough to be a manageable pet. It was company for me whilst living in another country without any family. I loved him, I loved him so much I wanted him to have friends. Those friends turned into his lovers and soon enough the result was born; my first move as an entrepreneur at the sweet age of seventeen was inveterate.

Unintentionally the puppies attracted a lot of attention, people had seen how much joy my dogs had brought into my life and approached me to buy them, It was the first time I thought 'I am in control of my life, I am my own boss.' It felt good! However, after four years of living a surreal and wonderful life in the sunshine on my own terms, I felt my time in Spain was feeling complete. I had had a lot of time to think about what to do next, I was considering coming back to the UK to study; I had saved 30k that year that would allow me to create a prosperous financial future when the time was right. Little did I know that moving back to the UK would result in being abused by someone who was meant to love me.

I returned to the UK and within a few months I met who I believed was the right match for me. He said all the right things and seemed to say them with sincerity, but it wasn't long before I realised that I wasn't in a desirable relationship.

It began with unkind words, ways to make me feel worthless; this was maybe one year into the relationship. Soon after, the hate speech was in public places. He would be jealous of other men even glancing in my direction, he would become very angry if I looked a waiter in the eye whilst ordering from the menu, or checking my mirrors whilst driving; he would accuse me of trying to attract attention from other men in their cars! It was just progressively getting worse. My earliest memory would be 1am standing in the kitchen, making a glass of water and seeing the lights of his car signalling his arrival home. Drunk and aggressive, he began his routine behaviour.

He was angry after a stressful day in business and to shorten a long story, he began smashing wine glasses and throwing them at me. After a few minutes I was crying on the floor surrounded by glass and bleeding. Of course, he felt awful, couldn't believe he had done such a thing. This was followed by gifts and loving actions, until similar incidents happened again, and again...

The physical violence and psychological abuse became worse throughout the years, and I felt I couldn't leave, I was afraid of what he might do. One day I tried to muster the courage to finally leave. I packed a small case and attempted to run away. Upon his realisation of losing me, he did the unthinkable...I ended up in a coma.

I was completely unconscious of my surroundings, in intensive care, with the possibility of not waking up. It was in the hands of my subconscious mind to keep me alive, or not. Thankfully, I survived, and I WOKE UP, but not just physically, I became fully conscious to what I needed to do, I felt tuned in, it was a reawakening.

I knew I had to become stronger and remove myself from this situation before it killed me indefinitely. Looking back, ironically the coma saved me. Without that chapter in my life I may not have been so determined to create something better for myself. It seemed less of a tragedy to potentially lose my life, than it would to one day lose the closest people to me. All that had happened was now the most propelling factor that I needed to set my positive future in motion.

I had already lost the beautiful life I had built as a result of my time in Spain, living in the sunshine and earning an amazing income in my teens from a business I built with pure passion, and saving more money than I could have ever imagined. It is most people's dream and now, following the years of abuse in my relationship, it was a distant memory of a life I had lived before. But I was determined to achieve my wildest ambitions again. I knew it meant catapulting myself out of the darkness once more, but this time I would create an even better life that I am in control of and that nobody would be able to take away from me. I continued my studies and professional development within Aesthetics and cosmetic procedures and business, and eventually I decided to open my first clinic.

Opening my first clinic alone was daunting and the first stages were the most challenging at times, but doing what I love the most as a practitioner was one of the main drivers that kept me working persistently for a minimum of eighteen hours per day for over two years, to build my dream of running a successful company and growing year on year!

I jumped head-first into business, taking massive risks and using all funds available. Of course, not yet business savvy, I had a somewhat naïve mind. I was young and perhaps in hindsight I would have made some decisions differently, however we learn from these moments and, if we make the right choices soon after realisation, we can use that insight for future conclusions. It took two years of minimum eighty-hour work weeks, zero socialising, zero frivolous spending and zero days off! I lived small, I took my cars off the road and absolutely everything I had was catapulted into my business, every penny.

Fast forward to my third year in business, finally with all the sacrifice, all the hours endured and all the decisions that led me this far, I hit a seven-figure ceiling. Now, many people I know would have been content with that, I on the other hand had a bigger vision, even greater goals and this wasn't my end point. You see, one of my goals is to create a life of time freedom, whilst still having a solid business. I wanted to create a business where I would not be needed daily but could oversee effectively. I knew I needed to expand my vision and think outside the box. if I was to make this happen.

I decided I was ready, and I opened my second business inside of the same arcade opposite my first business, I opened a hair salon. I had no experience in this industry – my experience is solely Aesthetics and business – but I did it anyway. It was new, very challenging and not how I quite imagined prior to investing, but I took the risk, I risked everything to grow my business, to reach closer to my vision, to step out of my content space with my first successful business and grow through the risk and fear of practically starting a new business from square one! Total renovation, hiring new staff, building a new client base, different marketing strategies, managing more of all aspects, higher outgoings, massive fear, but I took massive action to match it all.

I was back in the sacrifice stage, I was back to counting every pound, feeling that uncomfortable feeling and wondering once again if I had made the right decision. To this day I am still pushing forward with both businesses, working hard and staying focused on my end goals. Watching each of my businesses grow is something that makes me feel proud, when I think of where it all started!

The same year that I opened the hair salon, my partner and I took the leap and set up a third company, *Vployee*, which was initially to help my own businesses in the UK, so I wasn't stretching myself too thinly, to effectively manage all calls, emails, Facebook messages, Instagram messages, YouTube, marketing, posts and updates, outbound sales calls, content creation and so much more. Yet the amazing outcome has been the help we've been able to offer other businesses also. This one decision has been a game changer. One decision!

Of course, throughout all this time, there was plenty of peripheral noise, usually from the people that did not see or share my vision. The whispers sometimes felt like a thousand cuts, but if I listened to the doubts, the fears and the unnecessary noise, it would have put a roadblock in my way and prevent me from moving forward. Experience has taught me that one should always question how qualified someone is to advise you before taking their advice or criticism on board. If I had listened to the uneducated fears and comments of others', I would certainly not be as successful as I am today, or anywhere near it. If I had listened, I would probably still be in employment and daydreaming of a way out. So, I choose to only consider the information someone gives, if they are in a qualified position to give it. If someone has never tried, has no entrepreneurial experience or no knowledge of running a business, I close my ears. After years of experiencing this, I won't allow the negativity in to affect me in any way. Instead, I question anyone who questions me. Have they tried and failed, have they tried and succeeded?

I also tread in the circles of peers and professionals cautiously. As this too can sometimes be a frosty welcome, as we network and elucidate one another, and make assumptions; there have been times where I have heard the negative whispers of others where I realise I must stand strong and continue working in line with my core values and beliefs and not allow myself to give any energy to this misinformation being murmured by the uneducated, which unfortunately can become quite unrestrained and deafening to misinformed ears. Individuals close to me have ascertained first-hand the inordinate and inappropriate and objectionable blether. I must keep my mind in check and stand confident in the knowing that I am highly experienced and utterly confident and competent within my sector and others cannot deprecate or criticize as loud as my positive actions on a daily basis.

I will continue to push forward taking massive action within this industry, and I wish all who do the same the very best success and prosperity. I believe that anyone doing well must be working very hard and I commend all who endeavour to achieve; it's fantastic seeing others doing well and succeeding in life and business!

I have armed myself with self-talk survival and I go back to it, if I ever need to. What if I succeed? What if I grow even greater? What about the knowledge I'll gain? What about the experience I'll have? What if it's the best decision I will ever make? What if I don't do it? What's the worst thing that could happen?! Fail? What's failure? Failure in "learning". You learn from failure, you learn from circumstances that lead to failure, or rather how you deal with said circumstances in the future.

I have been on both sides of the fence. Yes of course throughout the years, I have thought to myself "they may be right". At one of the most challenging times of starting my first business, I had checked my bank balance and wondered how on earth would I stretch £42 for myself and my partner for over a month to live on! And then within the next month I hoped to break even. But I ploughed through and I am proud of the fact that I have experienced the true grit of building my own business. And I love to see others do well, as I know how difficult it is. If anyone is doing better than the mass population, hats off to them. They have sacrificed, worked harder and invested all their energy into a better future. It's fantastic to see others succeeding in life. I would want this for anyone who wants to better their life. If you ask me, being the best version of yourself, should be everyone's focus.

One of my goals is to create a strong future for myself, to be wealthy in my finances, my health and my life balance, to be able to help others and be independent. I want to know that under any circumstances I can rely on myself, just in case of the unexpected and unpredictable. If you are aiming to create the wealth to live the life you desire on your own terms, you must grow out of your comfort zone. Without a dream we have no focus and without focus we have nothing to work for. If we live in a plateau of standing still, living the same life daily over and over, until we refocus and decide to work on the unknown, results won't change!

A frightful statistic is that 1 in 2 people require long term care. Life expectancy has increased, disease is on the rise and it's unaffordable for many to live a life autonomous in retirement. And so, I made a decision to be financially free in my lifetime. The fact is the energy of wealth is global and determines almost all decisions in life. The smallest of decisions can alter life indefinitely. I will never allow myself to become complacent or to be arrogant to the fact that I know enough. I'm continually learning, I'm excited about learning, and I'm hungry for new knowledge. I feel powerful with it .

Everyone has a story, we all have moments of tragedy, where the choices we make are fundamental to our future. Never become unconcerned about yourself or your life happiness. I focus now on being the best version of myself, not on others' ideas of what I should be. I ask you to do the same, to become the best version of yourself. That may mean thinking differently about your life but it's worth it.

Imagine yourself at 150 years old, looking back at your life decisions. Are there any changes you would make right now, to ensure an enjoyable lifetime-view at age 150? What goals and dreams do you have now? Have a think about it now and write them down as they come to you. Then work on making it happen!

____

____

____

____

____

By investing in yourself and your own education, you can create security that nobody can take away from you. For example, I could lose absolutely everything. However, my knowledge and skill set are still readily available for me to always succeed, again and again, to duplicate everything I've learnt and regain my success.

The Importance of Mindset

My positive outlook on life and my ability to bounce back and work through fatiguing situations that feel unimaginable, is key to my success. My persistence and trying nature serve me well. No matter how tough things get, I always keep trying and don't give up, I've been that way since a very young age. Perfect practice makes perfect, and every minute, hour or day you are wasting being tired and not being persistent or focused on your actions, a secure future becomes less likely. Focus your energy on working stronger and conscientiously to ensure your future is safe and secure in the knowledge that you have put yourself in a position of wealth and continual streams of income by investing instead of spending on irrelevant possessions. If it's a need, you'll know. If it's a want, it's unnecessary. I'm so busy in my business and focus that I very rarely go shopping, and I don't feel the need to. As a woman I enjoy feeling confident and buying something to compliment my hard work, however I genuinely only shop for necessities such as business meetings, awards evenings and events. My businesses require my full attention, therefore general socialising isn't at the forefront for me right now.

To be financially successful, these lifestyle changes are paramount. If you look at everyone around you, that's your competition, and in that you will notice that most people have the same mindset. They will begrudgingly wake up for work on Monday, and by mid-week they are thirsting for the weekend. They will probably plan to buy a new outfit, discuss with colleagues and friends the "event" to go drinking Friday and Saturday, and spend Sunday hungover, unable to move from the sofa and dreading the work week on repeat. Be wiser than that. Spend your money wisely, and aside from your education (post compulsory schooling), invest in things that you will make money from, such as property, stocks, businesses, etc

Having a productive mindset has worked for me so it can work for you too, no matter what your starting point is. I feel everyone should feel free in life. I give my students the opportunity to create a solid future for themselves too. I have created a framework to teach my students how to succeed within the Aesthetics industry. My third company, *Vployee*, makes this framework possible, and is a way of helping people to cope with their business growth and plans of expansion.

I'm currently working on minimising my duties in the UK and focusing more on the opportunities on a global spectrum. This is a moment of change and, as I have already mentioned, any decision could change life and business on a massive scale. I'm not so naive now, therefore, I realise life can be unpredictable, but I am positive and more astute now. It's amazing what you can pull off when you are completely focused on your purpose and your goals. I believe your results are often determined by the direction of your energy. If you focus on the "CAN'T DO", it's difficult to find a "CAN DO". Without positive and passionate energy, you have nothing. Dreams are powerful, dreams give you focus, that focus will drive your passion, and that's where magic is born! The energy around your goals needs to be powerful enough to move you forward, whatever your goal is.

Sometimes energy can come from other people too, which can be a good thing or a bad thing, depending on who you surround yourself with. There is a saying that you are the result of the closest five people you spend most time with. I think there's a lot of truth in that if we take the time to truly look at it. That said, it's important to be around and learn from the people who match your mindset and will help you be in a positive place. If you are around people who are disinterested in you and your ambitions and you feel it is affecting your ability to function at your highest levels, then spend less time with them. Do not allow yourself to be dampened down by others' undermining comments, lack of understanding, lack of support, jealousy, arrogance or sense of entitlement. Be around people who raise your vibration and who care for your greater good! That may sound selfish but in fact being selfish (caring for self) is essential to your growth. Being self-centred on the other hand is not. The world does not revolve around you, but it does need you! And you can only be here, if you look after yourself.

Being the best version of yourself is your birth right. *Choosing* how you live your life is part of making it happen. I learned that the hard way. Of course, there have been times, and still are, where stress and people have affected me, even if not visual on the exterior, but I have a choice, as do you, to manage that or not. Apparently, human beings only use 10% brain power. Wow! Just imagine the genius within all of us if we only tapped into that switch to light up that remaining 90%. Can you imagine if you made conscious choices that support your growth and focused only on reaching your potential and tapping into that every day! What a tremendously wonderful place in time that would be. I have chosen to focus on reaching my full potential. And I have found that certain tools help me do it! I would like to share them here with you.

Write down five ways to clear your thinking and de-stress. What calms you? What helps you focus?

____

____

____

____

____

Visualise what you want, even if you don't have it yet. Imagine it and write it down now.

____

____

____

____

____

Write down five things that affect your clarity of thinking

____

____

____

____

____

Who are the five closest people to you? If any of these five people are side-tracking your vision, be conscious of it.

____

____

____

____

____

What benefits does each person bring to your life?

____

____

____

____

____

What are five barriers you see in between yourself and being free and successful in the area of life that's important to you?

Write five ways of lifting those barriers, imagining they are not there.

____

____

____

____

____

What drives you? Think about your WHY

____

____

____

____

____

The Importance of being Self-Aware

Self -awareness (the conscious knowledge of one's own character and feelings) is not something I always had but it is so important. Knowing yourself keeps your brain in check during the tougher times. Others may say or do things towards you that don't quite make sense, or hurt you in some way, but self-awareness helps you to refocus on the actuality of your surroundings. Ask yourself what you are feeding your mind daily. Are you nourishing or killing it slowly into degeneration? Your mind is a powerful source, however, if not managed it can take hold and control you into a frenzy of stress, angst and ill feelings. Imagine your thoughts, picture what you want to create. As human beings we need focus, we need to feel accomplished, and excitement helps. It's okay if you are not in the mindset you wish to be yet, it's okay to take time to gather your thoughts and determine the best path but do certainly try. As each moment that passes becomes a time of the past, start making your history count. Create a history that those to live ahead of you will be proud to mention you as a true attribute to the family tree. What do you want the future generations to remember you for? Make it happen!

My nine year in industry profile demonstrates my commitment to maintaining high standards and looking to continue working with industry leaders and professional businesses who hold the same core values as myself, which are key to my company's exponential growth plans. I came from a dark place but by becoming self-aware and having the right mindset, I am now in a position of positive influence. I am providing interactive training, and support to my students internationally, affiliated to the CPR Register, a register which allows for an unbiased approach with the opportunity for competent students to be trained to the highest aesthetic standards. These standards are deemed safe by an expert for the world Health Organization, Dr Dyakova, who sits amongst other world leaders who are also experts in their field. My board of certified experts oversees my work and deem safe my theoretical and practical approach to delivering the most comprehensive courses. I'm recognised personally in the UK and internationally, and my aesthetic industry presence amongst other industry experts continues to be viewed as a credible source of information with training content that is showcased amongst corporate and social media platforms.

The foundations of my philosophy are highlighted by the ongoing propaganda and lack of truth provided to the public and other professionals who are misinformed, leading to a judged perspective of the industry. Unfounded, unprecedented hierarchy is something I see almost daily, which is unfortunate to say the least. This is an industry within its own right, specification and speciality that deserves its own identity of qualification, skill set and, needless to say an eye for a positive improved aesthetic enhancement.

My work over the years has changed so many lives significantly. I have mastered the fine art of achieving beautifully natural results based on the science of the golden ratios of the face. Over the years I have treated thousands of people and helped so many who without my support have said they would have felt too self-conscious to even leave their house. I have worked with colleagues in Dubai and India who treat victims of acid attacks and babies born with cleft palate for no cost at all, an amazing charitable cause. This has been one of the most rewarding parts of my career so far.

Everyone has a story; life is a journey. We all have our own concerns, problems and choices to make. I feel so rewarded, to everyday be able to advise, guide and treat the concerns my clients have. Everyone deserves to feel confident in their own skin. My knowledge, expertise and empathy allow me the privilege of bringing out the best in someone who feels lost, allowing them to live their best life smiling from the inside out with new-found confidence. I treat many conditions that cause concern and lack of confidence in both women and men. We all need help sometimes, and I have made it my life work to bring happiness and a renewed zest for life to my clients. How I see it is that the more treatments I am able to offer, the more people I can help to feel better and increase their confidence daily. Some may still have the perception of Aesthetics treatments being a case of vanity, however, it is so much more. What I see daily isn't necessarily what you would assume to be the reality. I have found that many suffer in silence for many years before building up the courage to take the first step, however, once they have experienced the boost of increased confidence and no longer feel self-conscious or low due to something that would have otherwise effected their self-worth daily, it's truly life changing.

As part of the industry I am striving to continually raise the industry standards and to educate others to provide transparency, to ensure that all practitioners are working to their highest levels and under a framework, practicing at the same critical levels of theoretical and practical knowledge across the board, to diminish unfounded or fabricated versions of what they want others to believe throughout each sector. My goal is to achieve a harmonious attitude between all practitioners once standards have been raised within the cosmetic industry.

By the time this book is published for you to read, my life will have changed dramatically, I know this as it's a constant change. The events in or beyond my control and the decisions I make, continually change my life. As an entrepreneur I could lose everything I've worked for, overnight. You could be reading this, and I may be back at square one. However, with my experience, knowledge and positive light within me I know I will use everything within my power to become the woman who I aspire to be. I'm not there yet, I'm aware it will take years, yet I'm patiently impatient to be the best version of myself.

We define ourselves when we wake up in the morning and choose to either work out or stay in bed an extra hour. We define ourselves when we call in sick at work, knowing we could have gone in given it wasn't a crippling condition. We define ourselves when we work for others, never reaching our own potential. We define ourselves when we say yes to a risk that could change life in a great way or a negative. Every decision we make defines us every day. The quickest way to change your mind's focus is to change your surroundings and who you spend your time with.

I hope after reading this (I must admit a very condensed version of my story so far), it will help you to realise and understand that it doesn't matter who you are, what you are doing or what you think you can't do. The reality is, you truly can do anything that you want in this life. I believe we have one conscious life on this planet and the world we live in has so many wonders to explore. You are a plane ticket or a decision away from changing your life. You may not have had the most fortunate of beginnings, but your beginnings are now your past; there's always time to write the future you want and deserve. A decade ago, I would have never dreamt that I would be who I am today, at one point I believed I was taking my last breath. I promise you that everything can change with your will and courage to win!

Remember,

- Life is precious and every day is a chance to make new choices to change your situation
- No one must be unhappy, focus on your own happiness
- The smallest decision can make the biggest change to your life. Try it and see for yourself, it's true.
- Find a passion and do it well with high energy.
- Don't stay in a job you hate, apply for a new one or start your own business.

- Don't stay in relationships that suppress you or cause you hurt or pain, leave. There are seven billion people on this planet. Find those who match your vibration!

With Gratitude, Dr Pieter

I feel I owe so much to Dr Pieter and I wish to acknowledge him here, to me he was a teacher, mentor and friend. He was a truly inspiring person and offered so much support and goodwill from the early times of my business, until his devastating passing. Such a wealth of knowledge, the kind of intellect you couldn't find in a textbook, his drive to succeed and will to change negative aspects of our industry were motivating and of interest to so many.

His kindness to others was pure and his presence would light up a room. It was his courage in me that shone a high level of confidence and self-belief in me to continue growing my business and pushing harder to succeed. He introduced me to other experts in the industry, he connected me with international connections with whom I continue to work with to this day, he taught me so much invaluable information about business that I am so grateful for. He inspires me to continue working through all barriers that I come across to this day. Thank you, Dr Pieter.

Think Outside the Box

by Dorota Zurek

'Peace comes from knowing that good is all that exists'

With tears in my eyes I was looking at my beloved, my only child, Christian, suffering from enormous, abdominal pain. I felt helpless as a mother as I couldn't take his pain away. I was desperate. I was replaying his life in my head over and over to see if there was anything I had missed. Did I do something wrong that my son was so sick, that he couldn't even attend the school for nearly two years, due to the pain he was experiencing? Everybody around me was telling me that it was not my fault. However, I felt guilty. I felt very guilty as a mother that I failed my child, that I couldn't raise and protect my son from this illness, that he had to fight day-to-day pain as well as his everyday struggles with autism.

Christian's bowel problems got worse three years ago and eventually he had to be seen and admitted to the National Children's Hospital in Tallaght, Dublin 24. Despite doctors' efforts there was no straightforward diagnosis for his bowel problems and there was no cure.

Last November, after many months of constant diarrhoea, dramatic weight loss and terrible tummy pain, which was not possible to handle at home, my son was admitted again to the Maple Ward, in the hospital in Tallaght. He was completely wasted at this stage. His weight was critical as his intestines were not able to digest normal food. He suffered from malabsorption, so he was malnourished, and his internal organs were inflamed. I was devastated. Every time I changed his clothes, I held my tears back so as not to cry in front of him. His body was extremely skinny, his bones were sticking out, and his skin was rough and dry, but the worst was to see his enormous, swollen belly. He even had difficulty carrying it around. Doctors feared that his extremely enlarged colon would burst due to gas build-up. The quickest solution seemed to be a partial colon removal, but this surgery would have been too drastic for such a little boy. For these reasons, a feeding tube was inserted through his nose into his stomach to feed him in order to rest his bowel. The goal was to get him diagnosed and treated so he could go back home and live pain free.

After a few days I was told that my son suffered from chronic intestinal pseudo-obstruction (CIP), a rare disorder in which the intestinal nerve or muscle prevents food, fluid and air from moving through the stomach and intestines. The child experienced the symptoms of an intestinal blockage, however no actual physical blockage existed. Over time, children with CIP can become very malnourished because their gastrointestinal tracts are unable to absorb food and get nutrition. Unfortunately, in many cases, like my son's case, the root cause is unknown and there is no cure for this condition; there are only different treatments available to improve the quality of life, such as nutritional support therapy, pain management and small bowel transplantation in severe cases.

After receiving this diagnosis, I was heartbroken. I was desperately looking for the cure. I went through different case studies documented in the United States (I couldn't find any case study in Ireland), but in the end I felt more stressed because there is currently no cure for this condition.

Dr Shona Quinn, the main gastroenterologist in the National Children's Hospital in Tallaght made a decision to start food replacement therapy and feed him with Neocate only, an amino acid formula. No other food or drink except water was allowed. And all we could do was to wait and pray that without normal food his colon would start slowly to calm down and shrink to its correct size.

The Maple Ward became Christian's temporary home. I was getting up every day at 6am, starting my work at 7 or 7.30am, finishing it at 3 or 3.30pm with no lunch break and driving straight after work to see my son in the hospital. I was like a robot at my office and to this day I don't even remember what exactly I was working on at that time.

Everyone around me was asking me how I was able to function like this. Little did they knew that I was in the first trimester of pregnancy as well. But when you are determined you will find the strength to do everything, and my motivation was my son. He was my hero.

Being in the hospital is very difficult for every child, but for an autistic child it is even more challenging and scary, and I had to leave my autistic non-verbal child alone there. Autism is often misunderstood, and medical professionals are rarely trained how to deliver medical help to autistic people. For my son the most challenging part was finding a way to communicate his basic needs to nurses in my absence. He had to let them know that he was hungry or thirsty or that his diapers needed to be changed. Imagine how difficult it was for him to get his message across with no voice and how stressful it was for me leaving him alone at night. At the same time, I was struggling with the pressure of some of the medical staff being angry with me for not taking time off from work, as they didn't want to look after Christian's care. They didn't want to understand that I couldn't stop working as it was not my decision to make. I remained working full-time in the IT company and I felt an unspoken pressure and dissatisfaction from my managers about changing my working hours to finish earlier. I just simply wanted to be in the hospital at my son's bedside as soon as possible, rather than at business meetings or on conference calls, etc.

In this situation I could have become a victim to my emotions, but I knew that feeling depressed wouldn't help anyone, especially my son. Children easily pick up parents' emotions, which can affect their emotional and cognitive development. When children see their parents being stressed, tired, angry, upset or irritated, they cannot help but experience that negative energy as well.

It was very difficult to be happy at that time, but I had to be strong for Christian. Seeing me happy and strong encouraged him to fight for his health and cooperate well with doctors and medical staff. I wanted my child to recover so I had to ensure that I was positive enough to lift him up.

There's nothing good about living as a victim to negative emotions. To reclaim my power, I chose not to be a victim of the negative situation and my negative feelings and focus on one goal and being grateful for what I could. I understand being grateful in difficult situations isn't easy, but it definitely helps. Victims are helpless, hopeless and pitiable. I didn't want to be a victim. My goal was to get my son out of the hospital and help him to enjoy his life the best he could, despite his intestine condition and his autism. In order to achieve this, I had to ensure that Christian remained positive and happy despite being in pain, and despite being in the hospital. A positive mindset was my number one goal in the process of recovery.

I asked all my friends and friends of my friends on Facebook to volunteer their time for my son, to keep him company while I was at work, to simply cheer him up. I was worried that being alone would make him depressed. The response from people was amazing and exceeded my expectations. So many people were eager to help and contacted me through social media. Every day at least one kind soul was coming to my son's bed to spend time with him and fight his loneliness. Very soon his hospital room filled up with balloons, toys and cards with good wishes, and Christian started to smile again. After a while, his bowel slowly started to settle.

One day Dr. Quinn called me in and said that for Christian to stay healthy and to heal his intestines he would have to have a food-free regime from then on. Instead of food, he would have to take Neocate formula only. She also told me something that I will be grateful for all my life. She said that in for us to get our life back I must stop paying attention to his swollen belly and I must completely park the idea that he won't eat normal food. Instead I must get focused on the long-term benefits of a food-free regime lifestyle. So, I did.

Not long after that, I began to see that there is good to be found in everything that appears to be negative. A positively focused mindset allows you to take a control of what appears hopeless. I embraced a new way of life and I took control of what I could. My son started to live a food-free lifestyle, and as his intestines got better, his cognitive skills improved dramatically, and he started drawing and painting. My autistic son started to express his feelings through art and started to become more independent. Finally, he could go back to school after a two-year break and he could make new friends! He got his life back!

It is hard to find words to describe the joy of seeing my son being able to attend school, having a birthday party or simply having fun dressing up for-Halloween. Every time I read notes from a teacher in his school diary, I couldn't stop smiling. Everyday there was note left for me to let me know how much fun Christian had on that day. The most interesting thing is that one of his favourite classes is a cooking class. He gets so much joy from making food for others and he is not bothered that he doesn't eat himself. He is simply enjoying the process of preparing the dishes. My son definitely mastered how to enjoy the present moment and how to be happy about little things.

However, despite this, in the eyes of society my son didn't recover. He can't eat normally, and for most people, even professionals, my son's autism is considered a disease, a disease that should be cured rather than embraced as a new neurodiversity type. Even today people contact me by phone or through social media offering a magical cure for my son's gut condition or his autism. I am grateful for their concern and their willingness to help, but they don't see the magic of my son's life happening in front of their very own eyes. They are so focused on looking for cures and possibilities for my son to eat and function the same as everyone else, that they are blind to what's visible. What is normal after all? Who creates social norms these days? My son doesn't eat the same as everyone else, but he can still have a life, and that is okay! My son's autism is not a disease. It does not determine his character, or his path through life. He simply has different brain-wiring and he perceives the world differently.

We often live our lives trapped in a box where bars are made from stereotypes, fears and rules created in our head or forced upon us by the society. But what if you were to start to think differently? What if you were to start thinking outside the box? Can you imagine how different life would be?!

This is exactly what I did. My son can't have a pizza or a sandwich and his food regime may seem boring (he is on a strawberry Neocate formula five times daily) but if you look at this from another angle, you will see that these five meals are actually tasty (who doesn't like strawberry after all?), and they are nutritional.

My son is 100% healthy now. He can enjoy school and he is working on his most important role of being a big brother! It's all about how you look at things. In order to see the beauty of life you must look at things from different perspectives and implement positive strategies to make change possible.

The most powerful exercise that made me think positively and feel at peace was practising daily gratitude. I started with being grateful for every little thing that was happening to me, for Christian and my family. Then I started to be grateful for things that didn't happen yet but that I wanted to happen, so I was visualizing them. I did this when my son was in the hospital, I was working on feeling grateful for his recovery and visualized him leaving the Maple Ward and happily going home. People underestimate the power of visualization and gratitude; however, it is the most powerful tool to eliminate stress, rewire the brain and help with recovery. Of course, gratitude practices don't always provide a quick fix for survivors of trauma, but some studies show that the positive effects of gratitude increase over time and with practice help heal traumatic life events. Therefore, I would strongly advise you to add a gratitude practice to your life.

You can practice it in many ways, for example, a gratitude list or journal, practicing gratitude in your thoughts, sharing your gratitude with others such as a partner or a friend, or through art.

In the hospital my son drew happy things like his home, his dog Kaci, his garden, etc. and he was attaching all the pictures to the walls to remind himself about what was waiting for him outside the ward. Myself, I started to practice gratitude every morning by writing ten things I was grateful for in my journal and then at the end of the day I picked one or more things that happened to me during the day to be grateful and thankful for them as well. I am still doing this every morning. It is a part of my morning routine now like brushing my teeth.

From my experience, gratitude can certainly help with the healing process of trauma and creates more resiliencies to deal with future traumatic events or stress. I strongly encourage you to take time to reflect on what being grateful means to you and incorporate gratitude into your life.

It is also important to create a positive environment. I chose to absorb my mind with positive information. I read, listened to and watched only positive things which were helping me to create happy feelings. I started to spend more time with like-minded people, and I avoided engaging with people who tried to drag me down or who procrastinated about my son's future. Dealing with other people's judgements, assumptions and stereotypes is not an easy job, but there are few strategies which are very helpful.

Acknowledge and accept that people are always judging others because the human mind processes and reassesses new information all the time and it is an on-going process. I am judged, sometimes in a good way, sometimes in a bad way. Not everybody agrees that I trusted the doctors and let my son live his life food free. One day, one of my son's private therapists told me that I must stop being delusional and accept that Christian won't be normal and he will have a short life expectancy as he doesn't eat in the normal way, and in the future he will need a special home to live in. I was told to focus on his healthy baby brother instead. Can you imagine how much my blood boiled at the time? How upset I was, especially that it was said in the presence of the child concerned? That was the last time I went to that therapist with Christian. What's the point of attending therapy if a therapist is procrastinating about a patient's future and saying such awful statements? Many people forget that we are not defined by what our body does or does not do, quality of life is an individual choice. I teach my son not to let other people define what that means for him. This lesson is very difficult as people often mismatch the ability to talk with capability to think. In fact, people who can't talk have often lots to say and they get hurt when you say harsh things about them in their presence.

If you don't want to live in fear of judgment or others' opinions, remember the following rules:

- Judgment is unavoidable. You can't control the judgments of other people as you can't control what they think. So why worry about something which is beyond your control?

- Let them judge you! *'You can like or dislike me. You are entitled to form an opinion about me, and I don't fear being judged'.* It is very important to ask yourself: "What judgment do I fear?" Once you identify the fear, try to reassure yourself or find a way that you could manage the fear.
- Look closely at your own judgments. Watch yourself and the language you use in your own head about the others. You will notice then that this process is unstoppable; the thoughts are coming to our heads and are going away. Life is too short to be worried about other people's opinions.
- Think outside the box to get motivated and stay motivated.

My biggest motivation and inspiration is my son. He energizes me to be my best self. Every day I see his struggle, yet he is the happiest human being I know. He puts me to shame if I feel moody because I see that for him every day is wonderful, despite all odds he has to fight.

My son has taught me that recovery happens when you accept your deficits, learn strategies to help you with those deficits, and learn to love and value yourself. It reduces the suffering that comes from struggling against the unfortunate facts of life. Look beyond the facts and take one step at a time.

Many parents of children with special needs are surprised that I am so goal orientated because they sometimes feel too low, too depressed or anxious with their reality, that they forget about themselves, about their self-care; and for them it is pointless or unrealistic to set personal goals. However, setting goals is very important, especially in difficult circumstances. It is fundamental to change the situation you are in. If you don't set goals or visualize a picture of where you want to be, you will probably lose momentum and not get there. Genuine change will require sustained effort. That's why it's important to keep goals realistic and attainable! Progress demands commitment and a sustained determination to overcome obstacles and attain goals. It takes determination, effort and time to modify behaviour. In my case, I simply accepted the situation. I acknowledged the health problems my son had, I admitted his deficits, and I accepted the reality of his new life. I let go of disappointments and I focused on investing my time into my son's recovery. For a long time, my mum couldn't accept Christian's food free life, but I was determined to work hard on my mum's trauma associated with Christian's condition as well. It allowed her to let go of unnecessary worries and negative thoughts. Instead she started to enjoy her grandson and think positively about the future.

I don't know your story my dear reader, but if you are experiencing any type of difficult time now, please be assured that it is possible to have more joy in your life. I have learned that positive thinking can help overcome problems. Having a child with special needs is challenging but there are a few things that helped me a lot through my journey with my son Christian. Perhaps they will work for you too.

- Learn about the importance of giving yourself time. Don't be afraid to explore your feelings related to difficult situations. We live in the world where there is a pressure to feel happy all the time. Myself, I have learnt the opposite that I do not have to be happy all the time. I let myself experience all emotions. After all happiness comes from within and if you pressure yourself to be happy you can eliminate the source of happiness. Learn how to release internal blocks to happiness while feeling okay to experience varied emotions, whatever they may be. Cry when you need to but acknowledge the change in your life. Focus on learning what lifts you up and brings you joy but feel free to experience your emotions.
- Understand that personal worth is not determined by the ability to function the same as everyone else. Be

aware of your personal strengths and weaknesses and remember that different isn't bad, it's just different. I get angry when people perceive an autistic child as a lost child and show me pity. Whatever situation you are in now and whatever challenges you are going through, learn as much as you can about your possibilities. The more you know, the better decisions you will take for yourself or your child. Educate yourself about the solutions, for example, treatment options and do not fear to ask questions.

- Accept support and start interactions with others who are on the same boat as you for social support and assistance. It's okay not to have all the answers all the time.
- Let go of disappointments and expectations. What's done is done. It is time to move forward, plan and organise days and months ahead. Be patient and kind towards yourself.
- Create a list of realistic goals, prioritize them to keep attainable ones first but know your limitations so don't push anything too far.
- Try to be in control of what happens to you or your family as much as you can.

- Focus on the positive things and stay positive. Your mindset and attitude are crucial in day to day fight with your challenges
- Channel your negative or angry thoughts into happier and more productive positive thoughts. Don't jump to conclusions. Do not listen to negative people.

I'd like you try a little exercise right now so we can create positive change even as you read this book. Sit comfortably and think about the challenge you have right now. Write down your thoughts associated with it.

____

____

____

____

____

____

____

____

Did you use positive words when you were writing down your thoughts? No, well, the reality is if you're constantly telling yourself "I can't" you may convince yourself that's the truth. The good news is, that thinking can be changed. If you used negative words, replace the negative words with positive ones instead. Tell yourself you will do your best or that you will try your hardest instead.

____

____

____

____

____

____

____

Do you see the difference? Only use positive words when talking and push away all thoughts that aren't positive. Don't let negative thoughts and feelings take control over you when you're feeling down. You are in control of your feelings and thoughts. Even if it's only for a few hours a day, push your negativity aside and only focus on the good things in your life. Try filling your thoughts with words that make you feel strong, happy and in control of your life. Concentrate your efforts to focus on using words that summon up strength and success. Never use words that make you feel like you are failing. You have to change your thinking if you desire to have a future different from your present.

I recommend that you repeat a positive phrase to yourself on a regular basis. I repeated to myself that my son was recovering, and he was going to leave the hospital soon to enjoy his life. My son was also drawing his affirmations on paper and sticking them to the hospital wall to look at them every day. When you direct your thoughts towards positivity, it can help you to control your thoughts when you start to feel stressed, sad or anxious. This technique is used widely by psychotherapists.

Think now about things you want to achieve or are extremely important to you and write them down. Pick three from the list and re-write them on a separate piece of paper so you can carry them around with you and read them a few times daily. You could also stick the affirmations to the bathroom mirror. Every time you go to the bathroom to brush your teeth or wash your hands you will look at them and re-read them in your mind.

___

___

___

___

___

___

___

___

___

Forgiving yourself

When my son ended up again in the hospital, I had to leave the past behind us and no matter how badly things went there was nothing I could do to change them. You must remember that constantly beating yourself up about things that have gone wrong won't change them. You must tell yourself that you're forgiven for your mistakes and allow yourself to move on. Whenever I feel negative thoughts about the past coming up (that I didn't act fast enough when Christian was little to diagnose him quicker, that I didn't recognise the symptoms soon enough, etc.), I replace them with positive thoughts about the future (that my son will recover, that he is in good hands and step by step he will get his life back). I reminded myself that things could be worse. And you should too. No matter how bad things are, remember that they could be worse, and please be grateful for all the good things that are in your life now, even when it seems there's more bad than good.

I invite you to look closely at any challenge you might have right now and think of it as an opportunity. Sometimes even the most negative things in our lives help us come up with ideas to turn negative thoughts into positive ones. Look at your problems and challenges from different perspectives. Thinking outside the box allows you to get rewards outside of your reach.

For example, I realised that my career wasn't aligned to my circumstances at that time and it wasn't going to allow me to achieve what I wanted. Instead of settling for something I didn't want and feeling sad about it, I chose to think outside the box and brainstorm new possibilities. I needed to find something that might work better for me and my children. I could only do that by thinking outside the box. I also wanted to lift other parents up and share my experience as a special needs mum. From my very own experience, I know that thinking about what you should have done differently doesn't help. You must try to give yourself credit for what you have already achieved in your life, no matter how small, and look for what works for your life as it is now. You are an amazing human being, don't let circumstance or judgements stop you living your life fully. Be happy.

You Are Enough
by Monika Florczyk

October 14th, 2005, the day that changed everything in my life, or at least the direction of it. I was living in Poland, I had a job, I was planning for college and I had a clear idea of where my life was going. I'd have a family, a house, a job, marriage and children. Life would be great. That was until I got the phone call.

'Car crash, death, come home!', that was all I heard. My father was frantic. I will never forget the tone in his voice. I tried to make sense of what he was telling me. It couldn't be true. My brother couldn't be dead! He was my older brother and had always been in my life. How could he be dead?!

Walking into my parent's house was like a blur, people around my mum, my younger brother and my dad. My brother was gone forever, just like that, with no explanation from anyone. 'Why did it have to be him?' 'Why didn't I spend more time with him?' 'Why did he have to stay in the army for so long?' I played these questions in my head repeatedly. But there were no answers. He was gone.

A sequence of events followed, including the funeral, which I can't remember much of. It was all so surreal, but so painful at the same time. My heart felt heavy, like it had smashed into tiny pieces. I just wanted him back. I just wanted to talk to him again, to see his smile or hear his voice. But of course, that didn't happen. He was gone. Dealing with that was hugely difficult and although I did anything I could to lessen the pain, the void he had filled felt empty.

One of my friends suggested that I should come over to visit them in Ireland for a visit. I wasn't keen on the idea at first but on passing a travel agency one day I decided to go for it. I had nothing to lose. A two-week holiday might give me the headspace I needed. So, I bought a ticket for June 17th. It wasn't an easy decision because even though it was only two weeks, I was leaving my younger brother there and he means the world to me.

I landed in Cork airport with a limited amount of money, but I had a place to stay. The two weeks flew by and we visited every tourist attraction in Cork. It was the break I needed and although I only intended it to be a holiday, I decided to stay a bit longer. It turned into a permanent stay. I got a job in a pub, collecting glasses and serving behind the bar, and I've never looked back since. After a few months of bar work, I got a job as a sales assistant and a year later I was store manager, and with some time life had a sense of direction again.

I had a good job, which gave me an opportunity to learn and grow within the business. I met amazing friends and I started to have a social life, organising visits to places around Ireland at weekends. Having been through such a difficult time, it felt good to have some brightness back in my life. I was smiling again. Getting up in the morning looking forward to what my day will bring next. Days were filled with work, but I finally started to have a life again. I did my driving test and got a licence (a big decision for me after my brother's accident) and bought myself my lovely Ford Ka, in red (my favourite colour). Thanks to this car I could travel anywhere I wanted. I saw so many beautiful places, such as Dingle, The Cliffs of Moher, and the Wicklow Mountains — you can't put a price on experiences like that. My friends and I organised Christmas parties, Halloween and birthday celebrations I (love those memories) and of course normal days, filled with dinners, walks and coffees. It was like life was almost perfect — almost!

But even though life started to feel better, there was one thing missing, and that was love. Like many people, I wanted to find that special person that I could share my life with. Of course, that meant kissing a few frogs along the way but after some time I found my Prince Charming, "the one", the person I thought I would be with forever. We got married and we stayed married for five years, both committed to making it work. But sometimes things are just not meant to be. We entered the marriage thinking it would be forever but then life happens and forever takes a different direction, due to circumstances, people changing etc. I'm very grateful for the marriage and there are many special memories, but I suppose when you fall in love you justify things and idealise everything, sometimes things that you know deep down are wrong. You make excuses for yourself and the other person. I entered the marriage a confident woman, but day by day I felt my confidence dwindling, 'Why do you have to leave a mug in the sink?', 'Why can't you pronounce words properly?', 'The house should be cleaned more.', and my favourite one, 'You are so lucky to have all of this, considering where you came from.' On one occasion I remember sitting on the couch in the middle of my sitting room at Christmas time. It was perfect, there was a beautiful Christmas tree, songs were playing in the background and the room was full of happy people chatting to each other. All I wanted to do was scream, so someone would see that underneath it all I was unhappy, lonely and lost. Instead I remained silent, and with each day that passed, I felt more and more inadequate. I felt like a total failure. It didn't matter what I did, how much education I got, how good a job I had, how well-spoken I was, it was never going to be enough. There were some days that all I wanted to do was cry, not get up, just stay in bed and wait for the feeling to pass.

Many people think that if you look confident, have your own opinions, perform well at your workplace and have a great education, you must believe in yourself. At that time, I had attained a business degree, I had a well-paid job and I had quite a lot going for me in my professional life, but the truth is I couldn't have been more broken inside. I questioned every single decision I made and every word I said. It had nothing to do with me looking into different options or evaluating situations, it was all because I was so broken inside. I was afraid to make any decision. Fear was part of my daily routine. Imagine waking up each morning and thinking 'Will I be good enough today?' One time when I was ready to go out for a fundraiser with my best friend, Catherine, I heard someone saying: 'Did you put on little weight?' — BOOM! There I was standing in the black gown, with my hair and make-up done, crying my eyes out because I felt fat! To be honest, even if I was the skinniest person in the room, I think I would still have felt fat and ugly. I felt weak and I didn't believe I could do anything right. Even though I was only size 12 -14, I felt so fat (all in my head of course) that I stopped eating, sometimes starving myself for days at a time, living on coffee and cigarettes. I was determined to lose weight — not the smartest of ideas!

I was also terrified to make mistakes, nothing serious but I was afraid I would say or do the wrong thing. If I thought I said or did something wrong, I would automatically think that people would stop loving me, even my family. I preferred to walk away from confrontations than resolve them.

The strangest thing was my life in the eyes of other people was completely different, only my closest friends knew the truth. Inside of me there was a little battlefield, trying to figure everything out, but from the outside everyone saw a good, stable life, with no worries. Sometimes people filter others' lives through material things. It's all they can see. If you have a house, a job, a car and take a holiday every so often then you have no reason to complain or be sad. Now, don't get me wrong, I'm very grateful for what I had back then. There were many amazing memories, that I will never forget, but there was nothing at the same time. How bizarre can life be? People didn't see that I didn't know who I was anymore. It felt like I had lost every part of me that I had loved.

In addition to all of that I started struggling with other aspects of my health. It started as a small little pain in my finger. I thought nothing of it for few weeks, but when the pain got stronger and I couldn't sleep through the night properly, I had no choice but to go to the doctor to check it out. At first, they thought it was arthritis and gave me pain killers. They didn't help so I went back again and again until finally I was sent to get an MRI scan. The scan showed that there was a tumour on my bone. I cried tears of pain, I had sleepless nights and no amount of pain killers eased the pain, yet with a perfect life façade, nobody knew. You would think that would be my little wake up call, to maybe start thinking about myself, but no, it wasn't. I continued with the façade.

When you want something so badly, you will do just about anything to make it happen, so I changed, and I did everything to suit others instead of doing things I wanted. Imagine cooking a dinner, planning a lovely evening and even though everything looks great, you don't put your favourite vegetables on the table, not because you forgot to but just because someone doesn't like it! I did things like that quite a lot, and I got quite good at it. I changed so much I didn't know who I was anymore. I had no ambition, passion, drive or life about me. I was just a quiet, scared person who was easily manipulated. It felt like my happiness didn't matter. I didn't know what being happy meant anyway. But that was just about to change.

I woke up one morning quite early, about six months after my tumour was removed (thankfully it was benign) and I looked in my mirror. All I saw was pain, sadness and failure. I didn't recognise myself and I realised that this was not the life I was supposed to live. I remember thinking on that day that what I really wanted from life was to be happy, even though I didn't know exactly what happy meant. I just knew it meant something better than the life I had. It was the hardest decision to make. I knew that if I was to change my life for the better, I had to leave everything, including the friends that I had made over the eight years. I had to face the unknown and It felt like the day I left Poland to start life in Ireland, leaving everything behind and starting over. I don't even know where the strength came from to leave, but I did. I moved into a small apartment by myself and started over.

*

The minute you decide to take control of your life you feel a sense of relief — it's done, your new life starts now. I had to dig deep and look for ways I could build myself up, ways that I could build a new life, in the hope I could be happy. I made a list of what I want to do, and I knew that if I was to make the list a reality. The first thing I would have to do was to let go of the past. It was the hardest thing I had to learn to do, so hard that I couldn't do it on my own. I needed help. My beautiful friend, Catherine, was always in my corner (I'm not sure how she was handling my madness back then!) and I knew I could trust her. She was and still is my star. I could not thank her more for everything she did for me during my darkest times.

One day, as I tried to figure things out, I began complaining. Catherine turned to me and said, 'Monika, it's not all about you.' There it was, my AHA moment! It *wasn't* all about me, the world didn't revolve around me! Everything that had happened wasn't my fault and I should be grateful for what I had because there are so many people who never get a chance to turn their life around. This was my start-over and I had a chance to make it work. As a result of that statement, I began appreciating every minute of my new life and committed to making my new life a success, but on my own terms this time. I decided that above all else I would become happy.

I created a "to-do" list, hoping that it might help give me some direction at least. If I could do one thing, it might help me do the next. I started small but every day I made progress. I took it a step at a time, and there were ups and downs, but two years on I am now happy. Starting over wasn't easy but it was worth it. With a decision, commitment and one-step-at-a-time practice, I now know that everything can work out just fine, in fact it can work out great!

Now. I look in the mirror and instead of criticising myself I say to myself, 'Let's do this!' I look after myself more, I eat healthily, I train healthily, and my energy levels are so much higher. I feel so much better. I choose the day I am going to have. Living in Dublin has opened so many opportunities for me and I am confident to accept them. I can attend seminars, I can hop on the dart and go to Howth, I can drive to the Wicklow Mountains or just go and watch the lights on the streets of Dublin during Christmas. I do what I choose, and I have learned to value my time. For example, I started visiting my younger brother more often. He lives in Germany with his wife-to-be, Kamila. They are a very important part of my life, and every time I spend time with them, I'm learning that I don't have to be anyone else. I know that real love has no conditions.

Now, writing this I am sitting in a hotel and having a cup of coffee. There is a Christmas tree next to me and songs playing in the background. The room has lots of people in it – it seems familiar, given my earlier picture of life, but there is one difference, I couldn't be happier inside! This journey is just beginning of a great life ahead.

So how did I do it? What were the little steps I took that got me to where I am today?

1. Make eggs!

Making eggs as a first step may seem funny and making eggs may not be your specific first step, but in times of doing everything for everyone else and not taking care of yourself, it's easy to forget the simple things. I had forgotten how to make eggs the way I like, so it was the start of choosing to do something the way I wanted and realising I could do it — box ticked! So, keep the first step simple.

2. Talk to someone, if you need to.

I booked counselling sessions and what a great help that was. If you are struggling, getting guidance and sharing problems can really help. We talked about everything that was in my head, without judgment. It was so helpful. There was this stranger in front of me who listened and gave guidance without being pushy. If you need to talk, do it!

3. Find something you enjoy

I looked for something different than I was used to, something to try that I might enjoy. I found a coaching course, that I absolutely loved. I found out there are people out there who think like me, like the same things as me and are focused on making themselves the best version of themselves. I finished my Coaching Diploma.

4. Do something nice for yourself.

I had a coffee date with myself. I love my coffee, but I had to learn to go and enjoy it by myself, so I did. Every few days I had my little "coffee day". It was very hard at the beginning to take time for myself, but I love it now. What can you do for yourself?

5. Change what you need to change.

It took me about a year to move from Cork to Dublin. I did it because I needed to do it for me to make things work. It opened opportunities and new experiences. I always did what was the most practical for me, a stable job, close to home, with good pay, but I wanted more. I wanted progression, challenge and learning, so I changed my job. This led me to getting my HR diploma and later to my recruitment job, which I really enjoy. Moving to Dublin gave me an opportunity to move from a position as retail manager to a Human Resources professional. Who said when English is not your first language you can't get educated?! Not only did I pass my exams, I also went to work for one of the most respected recruitment agencies in Dublin!

6. Work daily on personal development

I learned what happiness means and I committed to nurturing myself as a person of value. Two years after walking away from everything that I thought was forever, I can honestly say it was all worth it. I was invited last year by a lovely lady, Jenny, who I met at my coaching course, to an event in Dublin called the *Women's Empowerment Summit*. It gave me a chance to see the amazing Donna Kennedy on stage. Sometimes it's still hard to believe, that two years ago I thought of myself as a worthless woman from Poland (as if where you are from, is a bad thing!) and now I'm writing a chapter in this book, a real book, that will be published alongside the most amazing women!

7. Surround yourself with the right people.

It can be very hard to let people go from your life, but sometimes it's best to let them go or limit time with them, if they aren't good for you.

8. Look after your body

Not eating healthily and not exercising resulted in me being tired, moody, and exhausted at times. It's important to eat properly and exercise. Do what's right for your body. You will have more energy and your mind will be clearer.

9. Trust

This was very hard for me to learn. Two years ago, I would have preferred to walk away from people and delete them from my life, just in case they would hurt me. The reality is people can hurt you, they may say things they regret, they may not always be there for you, but that doesn't mean they don't love you or don't care about you. Trust has to be earned but don't do what I did, pushing people away just because I might get hurt. When you lose trust in people, it's hard to let your guard down. The feeling of not being good enough doesn't just go away, it's hard work, not only for me, but for the other person as well. I questioned every person I let into my life, and every time I tried to be open, I would shut down, terrified of being hurt. Without good reason I would question why someone might have any interest in me. Now here is why – because I deserve to be loved just the way I am! I learned it's not about them. It's about me. I should love myself first. No one should affect your self-confidence. You are beautiful just the way you are. Trust yourself and be open to letting others earn your trust.

10. Fight for what you want

This sounds cliché but it's so true. If you won't fight for your own happiness, no one else will. I did so much to achieve some of my dreams (this book is one of them) but there is so much more to come. Remember, do it step-by-step, not everything at once. Create a list for yourself, make deadlines and make them realistic and achievable. You got this!

11. Celebrate Life

Celebrate every single happy moment.

- My family – even though we don't see each other as much as we would like, they mean a world to me. I am proud of my brother Krzysztof and who he has become. Soon enough he will marry an amazing girl and I have to say when I look at them, I can see what support and working together as a couple means. I also celebrate my mum and dad. My mum always says I don't tell her enough, that I always think I can do everything by myself, so I had to learn how to be open. Having family is definitely something to celebrate.

- Friends – if you have even one person who you can call your friend, it's worth a celebration. I have my little bunch and always try to make them feel special. I finally learned you don't have to be perfect to be someone's friend.

- My very special person. I met Gary. It's hard to explain how I feel about him because our relationship is so special and so different. He makes me smile and he encourages me to chase my dreams. When he puts his arms around me, I feel I can do anything, but not because of him, because I feel strong enough to allow myself to feel that way. I learned how to love someone from the start. Being completely heartbroken is not a great foundation for a relationship, but Gary showed me how you can love someone step-by-step. He is very patient. We enjoy having a coffee together, taking walks on the beach, watching movies and taking trips away. Gary you are my love and I know I don't have to say it but thank you for being you and supporting me.

- Gratitude. I'm so grateful for everything I have. Every day, I remind myself what I have done in the last two years and make sure I feel good about it.

12. Have Faith. Things are not always as bad as you think. Focus and things will work out. Focus on things you can control. I used to get so worked up about what people thought of me, but the fact is we can't control how other people think.

Be You!

We all have only one life and life can throw obstacles and take different directions, but we all have purpose in life, we just have to find it. It doesn't matter where you come from, how old you are, what size clothes you wear or anything else. All you need to focus on is you, because there is no one else in this world like you. You are special, brave, strong and most importantly, YOU ARE ENOUGH.

I would like to dedicate this chapter to few very special people:

Mum, Dad, Krzysztof and Kamila and rest of my family.

Catrin and her family for welcoming me to your house and making it home for me.

Tara, Gillian, Maja, Justyna and all my friends for being part of this journey.

Gary – for being you, love.

And one more person (S). I hope you are looking down and being proud.

I love you all!

Open to Change

by Alma Greene

From the age of ten success was very important to me. In fact, by the age of ten I had my ten-year goal plan laid out. I was determined to be successful and nothing was going to stop me. In hindsight, I didn't just want to be successful, I *needed* to be successful.

Looking back now, this need stemmed from an incident where someone I had always respected tripped me up on purpose and told me that I was stupid and that I would never amount to anything. Unfortunately, with the trusting mentality of a child, I believed them, and from then on, I felt I needed to prove them and everyone around me wrong. This incident was repeated on numerous occasions in my childhood and it just reaffirmed that I had to be successful. How others perceived me became my driving force to succeed. To be successful became the most important thing in my life.

It didn't take long until I figured out that my way to success was doing well at school. I was just an average student at the time, but I worked hard and because of this my teachers were very good to me, especially my Science teacher, Mr Dolan. I loved school and, because I was so studious, I got away with a lot. For example, I didn't like PE (physical education) but I was always excused as they knew I would be doing my homework and studying.

Creating a study plan and sticking to it was not a problem for me I had become very disciplined. I remember for one of my birthdays asking for a gas heater as a present as our house got cold at night and I would stay up until all hours studying to achieve my dream of going to college. I was focused on doing well.

As I worked my way through secondary school, I realised my next step was college. The problem was in the early 80's girls didn't go to college - they did secretarial courses - and a secretarial course is not something I wanted to do, but in hindsight it would have come in very useful over the years as I'm now a one finger typist! I wasn't sure what I wanted to study but I chose Science. My science teacher was my favourite teacher and he had even visited my parents at our home to explain to them the importance of going to college. So, I went to college.

It was an amazing experience, a real adventure. I have always loved books and study, so learning seemed like a natural thing for me to do. I blossomed in college, I loved the structure and routine and I finally felt I could be myself. Going to college was a big deal for me, there had been so many obstacles to overcome to achieve this dream. Firstly, getting enough points to be offered a place, secondly convincing my parents to allow me to go, and thirdly getting a grant to finance my time in college. I had achieved my first major goal in life, and this really boosted my self-confidence. I feel small successes along the way really affirm that we can achieve our goals whatever they might be. I started to relax a bit and enjoy my life at college, I didn't feel I was under the same pressure to achieve. I just needed to do well in my exams and get a good job and I now felt confident that I could, once I continued to work hard.

It was in college that I developed a real belief in myself and my ability to succeed. Once again, I had a good relationship with my lecturers being an enthusiastic student, willing to please by studying hard and obtaining good grades. But I didn't really know what I wanted to work at, my qualification was very practical orientated, so I ended up first working and then managing a small laboratory. Very quickly I was looking for a new challenge and decided teaching was my vocation. But once again I didn't feel I was in the right place, I just didn't fit in. I would get reprimanded by other lecturers for running around the place, the syllabus didn't change much from year to year and I was bored. The other problem was that I was overly involved with the students and knew if any of them were having personal problems. Now I felt that if they were having a really bad year personally, they should be allowed some slack when it came to their exams. This certainly didn't go down very well with my colleagues and superiors, so I would wander around the corridors feeling that I should be somewhere else. Then one day I bumped into someone I hadn't seen for years and we got chatting about my career path. Her advice was to simply ask myself that if money and what others thought about my career was not important, what would I do? That was the magic question for me. I knew straight away what I wanted to do.

I simply thought back to my first year in college. I had a keen interest in alternative therapies as I had suffered with sore throats since I was very young and had been on antibiotics very frequently. I was always told it was a virus, so when I started studying biology (part of my science course) one of the first things we learned (much to my amazement) was that antibiotics didn't kill viruses. I started looking at alternative treatments and started having different treatments myself, which I found fascinating. I decided that I would like to follow a career in alternative therapies. Now the great thing about being a therapist was that I could make a difference to so many people's lives and I would never get bored again, as of course every client was going to be different and would have different problems.

Also, there is constant learning as a therapist, something new to study and a better way to do things, which is something I really love. That was the start of my studying different therapies over several years until I was sufficiently qualified and experienced to start up my own practice.

It was also around this time that another major impact occurred in my life. I went to Paris and visited Napoleon's tomb. I found it amazing that someone could be so important to have such an elaborate casket. I came away with the thought that I must make a real difference in the world and be successful doing it.

When I started my new adventure of opening an alternative health care clinic over twenty years ago, I was so excited. I always knew it would be a success and I was very excited about it. The freedom of working for myself, choosing my own hours, working from home and most of all doing what I loved and getting paid to do it. Being able to help people and make a difference to so many people's lives was what I had been working so hard for the last number of years to achieve. I felt like I was floating on air. I fully believed that this was what I had been searching for and now I had found my calling.

Fast forward fifteen years...

I was working all the time, even when I was at home, I was still at work, well at least in my mind. I was always focused on the next goal, what else I wanted to achieve. I had to be successful. The problem was, in the process of trying to attain it, I was so stressed dealing with other people's problems that I had nothing left for myself or to give to my family. I had no boundaries and didn't understand how important they were. As a result, I was bombarded with messages by text, WhatsApp, Viber, Facebook messenger etc. This is before we think about good old-fashioned phone calls. Even when we went on holidays, I spent the first week not able to talk to my family and the second week stressed out about going back to work, knowing the amount of work that would be ahead of me. But I was successful, wasn't I? Didn't success mean hard work and stress?

I actually had no concrete definition of what success was for me, so of course I never knew when I achieved it, resulting in me always wanting to achieve more. I felt that I had to achieve everything on my own and this success dictated who I was. Of course, my whole self-worth was based solely on my level of achievement and success. I was very driven with complete focus on achieving my goals (with tunnel vision).
The result was that I became too driven and very rigid in my thinking - at what cost to my family and me? I had lost my sparkle and zest for life and it all became hard work, I found it difficult to

get out of bed in the morning and get motivated to go to work. I thought I had to keep going as I had so many people reliant on me and I needed to help. I was trying to fix everyone's problems resulting in me feeling the weight of the world on my shoulders. I just didn't know what to do to get balance back in my life. As the saying goes, I couldn't see the wood from the trees. Should I look at doing something different, or doing things differently? The more unhappy and stressed I became, the more closed off I became to change. How could this be?

The definition of insanity is doing the same thing over and over but expecting a different result each time. My mindset of needing to be successful was a pattern that I was unconsciously repeating over and over and unbelievably I was expecting a different result.

The Impact of Beliefs

On the positive side my drive, tunnel vision and great focus gave me the confidence that if I decided to do something, once I could see it achieved in my mind it was a definite that it would be achieved. My belief never wavered because I completely believed it would be achieved. I never questioned it, as in my head it was a given it was already on its way to me. Even though in reality in most cases I had no idea where it was going to come from or how I was going to achieve it, it was like every cell in my body believed it. On the negative side I just didn't know when enough was enough and when it was a good time to stop. I never stopped to think about why I was so set on being successful, why it was so important to me, why I was so driven. I just thought that I was someone who got bored easily and needed a new challenge. I never stopped to think if this need for success had an emotional drive.

When I finished in college, I got a job setting up a small laboratory and subsequently managing it, but very quickly I started feeling unfulfilled. I hadn't thought about training as an alternative therapist at this stage so, I decided to become a teacher. I could complete my degree at night school as it would bring me back in contact with where I wanted to be working and give me the qualification that I needed for the job.

Becoming a teacher then became my main focus. I thought about it and talked about it all day to everyone even when I knew they weren't listening to me. I imagined myself wearing a suit getting into my lovely car on my way to work. I totally believed it would happen and of course it did. I had told so many people about my desire to teach that when a part time position came up, I was told about it and subsequently got a position lecturing in a college. I think people would have done anything to shut me up!

I'll always remember turning up to teach my first class, I was so excited and nervous. I was lecturing in statistics at 9am on a

Friday morning. Now Thursday night was always the night students went out socialising so you can imagine the ones that did turn up were not in great shape. In those days we used a projector with acetates, and it took me two weeks to write up one hour's lecture. This was not as easy as I thought it would be, as well as my nerves at standing up in front of the room before all these students. After a while I got used to lecturing and it wasn't such a big deal anymore. But you've guessed it; before long I wasn't feeling fulfilled or satisfied anymore and so once again, I needed a change.

The big difference this time was I had been thinking about my future and what I really wanted to do with my life. I had been studying alternative therapies part time for the last couple of years, so I had a plan as to what I was going to do next. I had also been doing case studies at evenings and weekends and by doing this I had quite a few people who were recommending me to their family and friends.

I subsequently left lecturing to set up Amber Clinic, an alternative health care clinic, which developed into an Allergy testing clinic. I always knew it would be successful. I could see people coming to it from all over Ireland. My self-talk was "I am so busy I can't cope with the number of clients coming through my door".

It took no time at all until the clinic was booked up with clients as I had envisaged. People came from all over the country with all sorts of health-related issues that they wanted help with, everything from skin itches and rashes, digestives issues, and low energy, to name but a few. I was happy and excited about my new venture. I had finally found my true passion at work. I really loved helping people feel better and get the results they were looking for. Every client was different, so every day was different and certainly never boring. This suited my personality perfectly as I love problem solving and there were certainly lots of problems every day to be solved for my clients.

But what do you think happened? Of course, it got so busy that I couldn't cope. I am a qualified Kinesiologist and Homeopath and I was dealing with more and more complicated cases, the more complicated the better and of course I loved the challenge, but it was catching up with me. Needing to be successful spilled over into every aspect of my life, even my hobbies. Firstly, if I couldn't see a benefit to having a hobby, I wouldn't participate, I just didn't get doing something just for pleasure. Secondly, if I felt that I wasn't good at something, I definitely wouldn't take part. It has taken me years to understand that it's okay to just do something you enjoy just for the enjoyment of doing it. I now love to paint pictures in acrylics, I find it so relaxing. It's amazing really, you can't possibly concentrate on painting a picture and think about anything else.

The consequences of putting too much pressure on yourself.

I think we all know that a little bit of pressure on ourselves when we need to get a job done can help us to stay focused and get the job done on schedule. However, when the pressure is never-ending it's certainly not a good thing. I became a completely different person, I felt overwhelmed all the time and found it difficult to sleep, worrying about what needed to be done tomorrow. I started to focus on what was wrong in my life and was complaining all the time about the little things, instead of focusing on all the positives in my life. This was completely different to the person I had always been. I had always remained positive, even amongst the drive and focus. Not surprisingly, I suffered burn-out. It got to the stage where I didn't want to socialise anymore because people would be talking about their illness or someone else's illness and I just couldn't deal with it. I started to suffer with anxiety, which affected lots of different areas of my life, but worst of all was that I just didn't want to go to work anymore, I was just too tired and felt I couldn't deal with my own problems let alone deal with anyone else's problems anymore. I had certainly lost my sparkle.

The funny thing is, I didn't even realise that I was suffering from burnout. It wasn't until I overheard a conversation where someone was talking about me that it suddenly clicked what was wrong with me. But what was the solution, how could I overcome this and most importantly if I stopped working, what then? I felt I'd be a failure. The "I need to be successful" part of me had to be busy and productive every day. Eventually enough was enough and it just had to end.

The Turning Point

It's funny how life goes on regardless of what we do or don't do. Over the years when I had thought about making changes and taking time off, I thought the whole world would end, but of course it didn't. It doesn't stop because of how we choose to live our lives, whether we make changes, big or small. The days and weeks continue to roll on and tomorrow is always another day.

However, life was very different for me and in ways it got tougher. When I closed the clinic, I was mentally and physically exhausted and I didn't want to do anything. I just didn't have the energy or motivation to think about what was next. I had no vision in my head. Since I was ten years old, I always had a vision of my future in my head and now this wasn't the case. Well not a plan that I could see in my head and this is the only plan that I find comes to fruition for me.

My whole identity had revolved around my work and being successful; with all of this gone I didn't know who I was anymore. My life didn't make sense to me. What was I supposed to do with my time that could be productive in any way, or how could I

conjure up some sort of a plan for me to make some sense of my life again and feel useful? I was just going from day to day with no real plan and with no purpose. For the first time in my life I had no idea what I wanted to do with the rest of my life.
I had no success plan and no vision for my future. I felt I had no self-worth either. When I started to talk about how I felt everyone would tell me the same thing, maybe I was doing the right thing by just doing nothing for the first time ever. This wasn't really what I wanted to hear but I became resigned to the fact that I needed to take time out to recover.

I started looking after myself better, taking my time doing things instead of rushing around all the time. I started meditation practice every morning to prepare my mind for the day ahead. I found Pranic healing meditation on Twin Hearts invaluable. It calmed down my forever-racing mind. I found as the weeks went on that I felt more relaxed and less wound up. I started sleeping better and feeling more refreshed in the mornings. Recovery from burnout is funny really because once I started to feel better and I had a few good days, I would think *Fantastic, I'm better!* only to discover that the next day I would feel exhausted again. Often the exhaustion was more mental than physical but gradually the bad days became less until I started to feel like myself again.

Urgent versus Important

It was around this time that I got an invite to an event held by Pat Slattery. He spoke about life and an "Urgent versus Important" concept. This was a real eye opener for me. I suddenly realised that everything I did in life was "urgent", but I didn't really know what was important to me. I thought if something was urgent it meant that it had to be sorted out straight away. The problem was everyone had something that was urgent that they were looking for a solution for, and there was this endless supply of things that were urgent knocking on my door every day. So, I filled my days working and trying to sort out all these so-called urgent things. Some clients even became over reliant on me being efficient, so they would leave booking follow-up appointments until the last minute. Suddenly they needed an appointment urgently as they were going to run out of remedies and of course I always accommodated them. I had been living in urgent mode, not knowing what important meant. I had been spending my time putting out other people's fires and not looking at what was important to me and my family. I can honestly say this has been the most important thing that I have learned so far. I realised I needed to spend more time with my not-so-little girl who is growing up fast. I also realised that I needed to relax about what I was going to do with regards to my future work and that it would come to me when I was ready as it had always done in the past. It's so easy to become overcome with other people's urgency and lose sight of what's important to you. If you take away the urgency in your life, what is important to you?

If I was to be and feel happy, not just successful, I needed to place priority on the things that really mattered to me. When I was growing up feelings were not something that were thought of as important or something that we should dwell on. If something was wrong the advice was 'Get over it' or 'Don't cry over spilt milk, just move on and do what needs to be done.' The problem with this is that regardless of how I felt physically or emotionally I just kept going regardless of the consequences.

I began to realise that if I had been more open and communicative about how I felt, instead of keeping it all in my head, things could have been very different. Measures could have been put in place so that I could have had more work-life-balance, not just work and success all the time. My mindset could have been more open to positive change by allowing myself to be more open to support, not feeling I had to be so strong all the time or that I needed to save the world and do it all by myself. I realised that I must take care of myself and drop the harsh expectations I had placed upon myself. This realisation was huge for me.

Becoming Mindful and Self-aware

Mindfulness is a very popular word at the moment, but what does it really mean in practical terms so that it is useful in our daily lives? For me I feel stopping for a moment every day and paying close attention to how I'm feeling about what I'm doing is a good starting point. 'Is what I'm doing giving me that feeling of a pep in my step, and most importantly making me sparkle?' I really need to be doing something that I feel passionate about and at the same time gives me a challenge.

I've learned that I need to have boundaries, something which certainly didn't exist in my life up until this point. Because I had no boundaries, I had no clear cut-off point with people and because of this, they felt they could contact me at any time using whatever means they wanted to use. By allowing this to happen it escalated into people arriving with no appointments and feeling entitled to my time. They felt they could arrive late, make excuses that they got lost and would still expect to be seen, resulting in no time for lunch and very little time to eat during the day. While I had a belief system of once everyone else is okay, it doesn't matter about me, things were not going to be any different. I had to realise that I also mattered, and that my family mattered. The way I felt had a major impact on my family life.

I've learned that instead of being the yes-person that everyone knows, I now take a moment and pause when I'm being asked to do something, to really think about it before committing myself. This is an invaluable little tool that helps to keep me from becoming overwhelmed by the things I have committed to everyday, and subsequently stops me from over-committing myself.

I've also learned that success can come in many packages and not all of them equate to finances or how the world views us. I now feel there are many more ways to be successful outside of the business world. For me being emotionally available for my child and husband when they need me, being happy and relaxed when spending time with your family and friends, is success. Just being happy with yourself is a major success in and of itself. All of this is much more easily achieved when you are looking after yourself instead of running ragged after everyone else.

So, after about a year of doing very little I decided I was ready to open Amber Clinic again. It was an easy transition as the phone had continued to ring during my time out. One Saturday morning the phone rang and when I answered it, it was a past client whose daughter was ill and wanted to know would I see her. I said Yes and that was it. This time it was different, I don't over-book or over-extend myself. I have my sparkle back and I feel excited about seeing clients and making a difference in their lives once again. I now recognise the importance of having regular check-ins with myself to see how I'm feeling and what I really need. A very important question that I ask myself regularly is 'Is this working for me?'

I still set goals but now it's different, the goals are for me and what I want to achieve instead of running after success with no end in sight. My goals are much more realistic and balanced, so I now have a good balance of work, family and me-time. I have learned how important it is for me to be able to do nothing and to enjoy doing what's important to me. I no longer tie myself to other people's expectations and I have more realistic expectations of myself. My mantra is based on two questions: 1) Is this working for me? and most importantly 2) Is this urgent or is it important?

It's a fantastic feeling not to need outside validation and to know that I am successful in my life. The fact is none of us need outside validation but sometimes because of the pressure of life events we put pressure on ourselves to achieve validation. You just need to realise that it's okay to be good to yourself, treat yourself with the love and respect that you so truly deserve, and have realistic goals and dreams that are really yours. Remember, it really doesn't matter how others perceive you. I think most people are so busy worrying about themselves that they don't give much thought to other people. So really the only person you really have to answer to is yourself. My advice to you is to always pause and ask yourself is this urgent or is it important.

Accepting Support

by Karen Keenan

'No man or woman is an island.' I remember the first time that was said to me. I had heard the saying before but this time it was directed at me. Donna Kennedy said it to me the day we were all brain storming about the book and it really hit home. I suppose I was never aware of how much I had closed myself off to people or situations. I see now that it was a coping mechanism for times when I struggled in a situation or when I didn't feel comfortable. As a type of self-preservation, if I found myself in a difficult situation, I would throw up a huge shield in front of me and if you tried to get to me, I'd raise the shield higher. I never liked to admit when things got to me, until it was too late, or I had become overwhelmed or burnt out completely. Donna held that mirror of reality in front of me and this time I had no choice but to look at it. It became obvious to me that shutting people out had become a destructive pattern in my life and trying to do everything on my own was an issue I needed to resolve.

When I found out I was pregnant with my daughter, Lydia, I didn't tell anyone who the father was, he didn't want anyone to know. I didn't even tell my family for a long time. I believed I could do it all alone, keeping the secret of who he was, and that it wouldn't affect me. I was wrong; it just started to eat me up inside and my whole personality changed. I became more anxious and uneasy, as I tried to hold myself together, knowing that I was lying to people. I was afraid of letting the secret slip, but I knew I couldn't continue lying to everyone. Before the secret I was someone who was open about everything in my life. I was very honest and never felt like I had to hold anything back from anyone. I was confident, I knew who I was, and I was very encouraging to others. I could literally feel the weight of that secret on my shoulders. I thought withdrawing from people would make it easier, but it did the opposite. I lost my confidence and my ability to believe in the support of others. I became very critical of myself and thought that if I gave myself enough of a hard time, I wouldn't be affected by other people's words or ideas about me, as I had already covered all areas before they were able to. I convinced myself that life would be better by myself and it would allow me to avoid the risk of being rejected or let down by someone else. I felt alone.

I could blame people for the feelings I felt of abandonment, judgement, dislike, shame, guilt, annoyance, being a burden, a torture and a hassle (the list could go on), but I've realised in a short time that the person who affects me the most is actually myself. I've learnt that carrying an impression of myself built on what other people thought of me and dwelling on their fears and worries only had harmful repercussions. To try and please other people can have major effects on your self-worth, self-respect and self-belief. I suppose I had suffered a type of "imposter syndrome" and the consequences weren't good.

I made a choice, that choice was to keep my baby, regardless of the circumstances and regardless of others' preferences, and I suffered the consequences of making that choice for some time. Keeping secrets and holding back on the truth can eat away at you and damage your wellbeing. I was just so afraid of the judgement that may come with letting people know the truth. I didn't know what to do or how to go about telling people the truth, given the fact I had lied about it initially. It's very hard to backtrack on a story without feeling foolish. But I knew I couldn't continue that way, something had to change.

Eventually I decided to tell my family and friends. It was difficult but I couldn't keep it to myself anymore. To my surprise, everyone I told was very supportive of me and they convinced me that the best thing to do was to be honest, that the truth needed to come out. They felt Lydia's family needed to know she existed so they could make their own choices in the situation. This was a decision that was also made for the sake of Lydia's future. She would need to know the truth at some stage and no matter what, I could never lie to her. She is a blessing in my life. Telling her young was the best thing to do.

When I started to tell the truth to the people closest to me, I was taken aback by their reactions and support towards me. They weren't really that concerned about the situation and I had unnecessarily worried myself about their reactions and opinions, more than my own wellbeing. I had created a whole situation in my head of how they saw me, assumptions that weren't true. My family and friends could not have been more supportive and understanding about the whole thing. I had just become so wrapped up in how others might perceive me that I didn't see the possibility that they might be supportive. I suppose when you are in your thoughts only, things can get muddled and you can view the world through a muddled filter, not the reality of what is or what could be. It's only when you allow people to help you that life becomes less overwhelming.

In September 2018 my dad was diagnosed with terminal lung cancer. He was given a diagnosis of three to four months to live without treatment or six months to one year with treatment. Unfortunately, he never got the chance to get the treatment. He passed away on the 18th of December 2018. Without the support of my family and close friends at the time of his illness, the time of his death, and throughout my own personal grieving process, I honestly don't know how I would've got through it all.

I was my dad's only child and he depended on me quite a lot over recent years. I loved him, and to lose him left a huge void in my life and throughout the first year of his death I felt very lost and confused. To lose the love of someone so close is devastating. My relationship with Dad wasn't perfect, we had our moments, but we also had such a close bond and a great friendship. We were able to chat with each other for hours on any topic or subject. Thinking about it now, we were so alike. When I made the decision to open up about Lydia's dad, Dad was still alive at the time — we didn't even know he was sick — and he was always good to chat with about a difficult situation. Even now I miss his love, support and understanding and the opinions he had of me. I miss the role that I played in his life and I have a genuine sense of loss within myself because of that. I take comfort in the thought that my dad is in a better place now because when he was alive, he fought a lot of his own demons regarding alcohol and negative thinking. I know he is happier where he is now, and I have huge faith and belief in God, as did he.

Throughout my Dad's illness and following his death my own health was deteriorating. I developed rheumatoid arthritis, anaemia and gluten sensitivity. In the grand scheme of things none of these ailments were life-threatening per se but because I was in such a low place emotionally, I wasn't dealing with or acknowledging them. I began shutting people out again and my health got worse. I was forever tired, exhausted, sleep deprived, anxious, depressed and unmotivated. Trying to change that on my own proved difficult. There were days I wouldn't go to work. When I felt very anxious, I would get paranoid, not wanting to leave the house. I started to withdraw again. Thankfully, a good friend of mine inspired me to start taking care of myself and to get out there within the community and help support others. A step at a time, I came out of my shell and it was a positive move in the right direction. I started looking for support in as many positive connections as possible. I got myself out there slowly, very slowly at the start and was very hesitant at times, but I kept going and the people supporting me were amazing and they still support me now. They gave me the influence, inspiration and courage to start helping others as best I could too.

I now understand that all human beings need communication, community and support to survive. As a society we have progressed in so many ways when it comes to technology and the advancements within industry and laboured work but in ways these changes have left us disconnected and disassociated, so we need to find new ways to connect and support each other within a community. Isolation is not conducive to good mental and physical health. To be healthy, we must allow ourselves to connect with other people, not shut them out or detach.

I heard a story on the radio not so long ago about a village in Africa where they installed washing machines in various homes. Following the installation of the machines, the women who usually washed the clothes started to get depressed. It soon became apparent that the washing machines were having a serious social effect. Up to that point the women went to the local river to wash their clothes. They were there together and socialising with each other as well as washing clothes. With the machines installed, they stopped going to the river and as a result there was a loss of communication, community and support within the group.

Sometimes it can feel overwhelming to create support and connection within a community or group, if you have lost it or never had it. I found it very hard at the start to get out there as my thoughts and actions for so long had created such a negative barrier and I was convinced I was unlikeable and unworthy for people to want to help me. One of my biggest fears was to be let down by others, so I didn't ask for help when I needed it. I now understand that *everyone* needs support at times. It is in our nature to be connected as human beings. To isolate yourself as I did, goes against nature. Never feel that you have to figure things out all by yourself. It's not a weakness to need help. It's normal to need help. And there are people willing to help and support you, if you just ask and be open to it.

I changed things around by taking small steps in the right direction using online community groups to discuss different topics, issues and then getting support back from ladies within the group. Then I went to a few personal development seminars and I began to realise that other women and men felt just the same as I did. I wasn't alone.

Life had thrown a few curve balls my way and things I had planned out in my early 20's didn't happen the way I thought they would, but that was okay and what's more, it was okay not to be okay. Life can present challenges, but it also gives us an opportunity to grow from them. It's only when we stay stuck and alone in challenges that problems occur. It was time for me to move from feeling stuck and start progressing with my life and to accept the things that had happened. Holding myself back and beating myself up was not going to undo or change my circumstances. I had to create new circumstances and I could only do that, if I let go of that isolation and disconnection mindset. I also needed to forgive the people who had hurt me along the way and forgive myself too. Forgiveness can be such a hard thing to do but it is so powerful when you do it. It gives you an awareness and that is an amazing tool to have. I have realised that over the years I have been judgemental towards other people and may not have taken a person's feelings into consideration. In my own set of thoughts, I could be abrupt, impatient, and ignorant to the fact that other people may see the world differently to me and that it is okay. I'm learning to appreciate the thoughts, ideas and feelings of others and to be more mindful of people and situations around me. I would never have intentionally tried to hurt or offend anyone, but I had created a pattern of detaching myself from situations. By developing some self-awareness, self-discipline and patience, I see things from a more productive perspective now. I am finding out that supporting yourself, gathering your thoughts and becoming mindful of your actions are major factors in discovering an attitude of self-care and self-love within yourself. I take it a step at a time now, and I am happy to say that I've learned to find the magic of everyday life. Importantly I am happy to let people in so we can share that everyday magic.

How to discover the magic in everyday life.

- Be forgiving. It will serve you well. To be unforgiving is like drinking poison and expecting the other person to be sick! Forgiveness brings calmness.
- Be encouraging. Stop judging yourself and criticising everything you do. It's okay not to have all the answers right now.
- Be flawed. Stop trying to make everything perfect and obsessing on perfection; nothing in this world is perfect so you will only set yourself up for disappointment. Strive for progression rather than perfection and be proud of

the person you are, warts and all, because we all have them.

- Be genuine and true to yourself. Don't compromise who you are to feel accepted by others. Work on your beliefs, values and integrity and don't let another person influence or manipulate you for their own interests.

- Be kind but don't be taken for granted. Always know your boundaries and put *yourself* first so you can be strong for others too. Compromising yourself isn't healthy.

- Be patient. Life has a funny way of working out. It might take a while to get to where you want to be, and that's okay, take the time you need. Everyone is on a different path so don't compare your journey to someone else's

- Be authentic. Be you! Learn to love yourself to the best of your ability. Take time out for yourself and discover who you are without all the labels. E.g. employee, mum, sister, daughter. You are you; a label is secondary.

- Be the best you can be and continually look for new ways to reach your potential.

- Accept support when you need it. No man or woman is an island!

A Life of Purpose and Meaning

by Una McGoey

"The purpose of our lives is to be happy."

— Dalai Lama

I was sitting on an Aer Lingus plane over Long Island Sound. I could see the lights and skyscrapers towering up from the ground. Flying over New York City gets me every time, I love that city. I arrived in New York on a June afternoon in the early 90's on my Morrison Visa. From a young age I just knew I was going to live there, I can't explain it, it was a knowing I had.

As I had no job, I was very grateful to have relations outside the city who were willing to let me stay with them for a few weeks until I got sorted with work and started to earn. Within days I was on the train into Manhattan with a folder full of one page resumes ready to hand out to every recruitment agency I could find.

After two weeks of unsuccessful job hunting, I attended a party hosted by my cousin in Connecticut. At the party I was introduced to an Irish lady who was working in an Irish bank in Greenwich. I mentioned that I was job hunting, and she was happy to take my resume to her HR Manager the next day. Within a week I was interviewed and started my twenty-three-year career in the Bank the following Monday. A week later I replied to a classified ad in the Irish Echo, which secured me a shared apartment for the next three years.

I enjoyed all aspects of the New York culture and made wonderful friends. We spent weekends skiing in Catskills, going to the beach on Long Island, concerts on Jones Beach and nights out in the city. I enjoyed working in the bank immensely and my "bank family" were fantastic. At the time I joined, there were only nine staff. However, when I was leaving there were over thirty staff employed. The company was growing, so it was a very exciting time to be part of the team. The experience I gained throughout my years in the US Bank was a great foundation for my continuing career within the banking system in Ireland.

As the news was breaking of Princess Diana's untimely death, I was packing up my apartment to return to Ireland with my beautiful six-week-old son. On the morning of the flight home my doctor diagnosed me with pleurisy, he recommended that I didn't fly home and a few hours later I was landing in Dublin Airport.

Luckily, I was still employed by the Bank and on maternity leave, but the only position available to me was in Head Office in Dublin, 70km from home. I had no choice as a twenty-five-year-old single mother with the responsibility of a new baby, but to take the job. This involved a four hour commute every day, leaving home at 6.30am and returning after 8pm. I was blessed to have the unwavering support of my wonderful parents and extended family, this was not the most common situation at the time. Luckily, after two years I secured a transfer much closer to home, making life a bit more manageable.

Just as I thought life was moving in the right direction, structures within the business banking industry were changing and I had to reapply for the role I was currently working in.

I will never forget the day I was called into my manager's office to be told that I didn't get my own job and to add insult to injury my work colleague, in the same office, was promoted to the position.

"You will face many defeats in life,

but never let yourself be defeated."

– Maya Angelou

I felt shell shocked, I just couldn't believe this was happening. I felt completely humiliated in front of my work colleagues and I felt like a complete failure.

I left the building and drove to my Aunt's house, cried my eyes out, had a cup of tea, dusted myself down and returned to work that same afternoon. Later that day, my boss called me into his office to say how impressed he was at my resilience and loyalty; for that I was grateful. Within days I was reassigned to a different position within the bank in the local branch.

I started a new journey in the banking world, starting on the customer service desk advising customers with their queries and their day to day banking needs, subsequently moving into advisor roles helping customers with specific needs, from savings advice to their borrowing requirements. As the years moved on, I progressed through the ranks taking on various roles throughout the system, gaining experience in all aspects of the financial world both personal and business banking, while at the same time undertaking professional exams. This helped me secure a number of positions, from Mortgage Advisor to Business Advisor roles. Ten years after arriving back from New York, I was appointed to my first Branch Manager's role.

Life at the time was very busy, taxiing to football and tennis matches, golf and all the usual activities of a twelve-year-old, while working a full-time job in a busy management role and juggling both successfully.

Around the *same* time my sister was attending a local parenting class and an Enneagram class, which she had recommended to me many times. As my son was going into secondary school, I didn't feel it was of any advantage to me. I thought it was too late for a parenting course. My sister persisted and encouraged me to attend. I actually hung up the phone on her, I resisted so much! After much persuasion I reluctantly registered for the class; little did I know that that was the start of my self-development journey and great changes for me! I attended the parenting class and realised very quickly it wasn't parenting for your children, it was parenting for yourself. I continued with the classes, Enneagram course, Myers Briggs and a second part of Enneagram.

Having discussed these courses with my manager in work I was subsequently asked to move from a Branch Manager role to a new coaching role within the region. I progressed into this coaching role, coaching staff and coaching managers to help grow their business within their branches. This was my first introduction to training and coaching, and it is something that I thoroughly enjoyed, and which resonated with me. This leadership role offered me the opportunity to do leadership programmes within the bank, which then led me to undertake a postgraduate course from Coventry University, in Leading and Managing People.

All the knowledge and experience I had gained over the past number of years eventually led me to question myself as to what I wanted out of life. What was going to give me future happiness?

My realisation was that my core values were not in alignment with the culture of the industry I was working in convinced me that the time was right for me to change the direction of my life. I took a deep breath and left my permanent pensionable job in the bank, stepping way out of my comfort zone! Looking back, I realise that the time, commitment and stress while working full-time, attending evening and weekend lectures, submitting assignments, sitting exams and raising a child prepared me to start my own business as a Coach, Mentor, Trainer and Consultant. I now help leaders and potential leaders gain clarity, deepen their understanding of themselves through personality profiling, while helping them to develop their leadership skills.

"Our WHY is our purpose, cause or belief, the driving force behind everything we do".

- *Simon Sinek*

Setting up my own business was one of bravest (not to mention riskiest) things I have ever done. I never thought it was going to be possible. It was never a good time to start, but I was advised to 'start before you are ready because it will never be perfect.'

I learned a very important lesson while working, which was to move out of my comfort zone and into my growth zone. It helped me set new goals and challenges and helped me find purpose and meaning in my life.

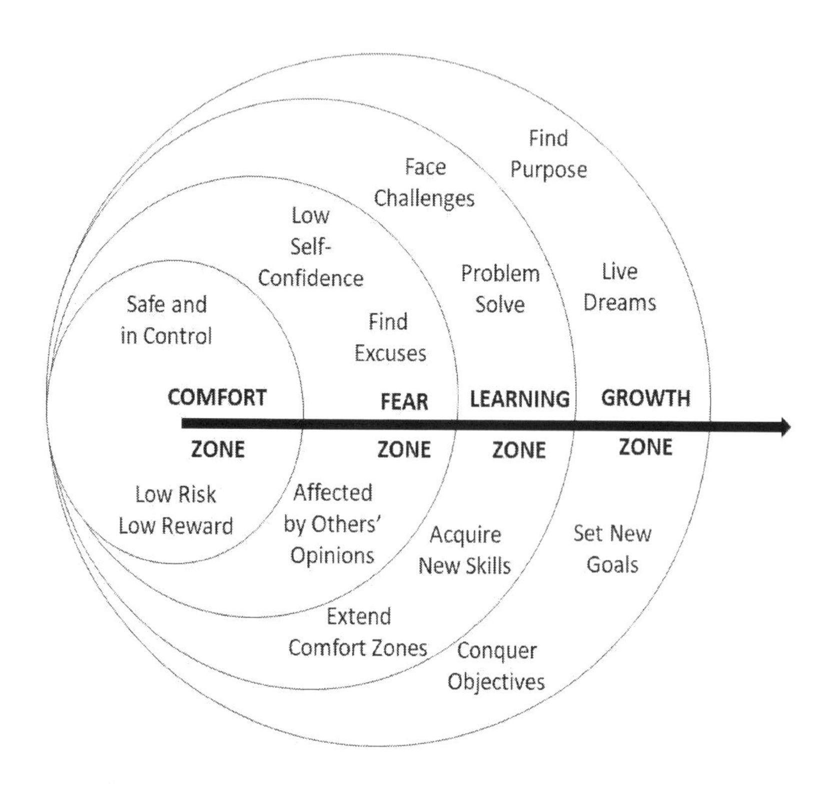

"If you want to live a happy life, tie it to a goal, not to people or things."

– Albert Einstein

One area in my life which I feel is important and that I love sharing with other people is setting goals. It helps me stay focused on what I want to achieve, and it also gives me a sense of achievement and satisfaction when I reach the goals. It's an ongoing process for me and my goals are set monthly, weekly and daily. When I'm setting my goals, these are some of the questions I ask myself. Take some time now to answer these questions for yourself.

What do I want more of?

____

What do I want less of?

____

What is important to me?

____

What new things do I want to do?

____

Where do I find happiness and joy?

____

What if I knew I could not fail what would I choose to *be*, to *do* and to *have*?

____

I prioritise my list by choosing the top two or three goals I want to work on this week or month. Once I have listed out my goals, I begin a *SMART* process, *Specific, Measurable, Achievable, Realistic* and *Timely*. I set my goals every month and I am still constantly working on them. The journey to success will always begin with the small step of taking a chance. Small steps = Big Changes.

"The journey of a thousand miles begins with one step."

– Lao Tzu

When I left my career in the bank I honestly felt at a total loss. I thought I didn't know, even after all my self-development courses, who I was. I was always known as "Una from the Bank" or "Una the Bank Manager", so I felt a huge loss of my identity. That was my life, I poured my heart and soul into it and I did my very best every day. I gave my job one hundred percent. This was all new to me. What was I going to do? Was I going to get another job? I knew I would need a hip replacement at some stage in my life, and after a Camino walk in 2013 the pain was really starting to impact my life. I decided to go ahead with the procedure in August 2018. When I was being wheeled down to the operating theatre, I started to laugh and cry at the same time!

Thankfully, the operation was a success and after a longer than expected recovery, due to a previous operation when I was born, I fully committed myself to starting my business. My first steps were to complete my coaching accreditation, psychometrics assessment training; emotional Intelligence and DISC Personality Profiling, in order to get ready for my journey ahead as a business owner.

I now love sharing my knowledge and experience, helping businesses to flourish and helping their owners and leaders to reach their full potential, to realise their ambitions, making positive changes in their lives. The journey of success will always begin with the small step of taking a chance.

These are some of the steps I undertook before I fully committed to setting up my own business.

1. I attended courses, talks, workshops and conferences which were of interest to me, usually personal development courses at weekends and in the evening time.

2. I spoke to other people in the industry, had plenty cups of coffee with them and asked questions. What worked well for them? I found people were so open, friendly and delighted to share their wisdom with you or make an introduction to the right person.

3. I took time out away from work to set my goals and identify what I really wanted from life. I scheduled time in my diary, stepped out and took time to figure it out. I started attending a meditation class, which gave me space and time to allow ideas to flow!

4. I identified and wrote down my values; there is no point in looking for a job in an industry where your values are not aligned. An alignment between your career and your core values produces satisfaction, a sense of happiness and fulfilment. A misalignment can cause everything from minor problems to major disruptions, such as leaving your role. My core value is loyalty and I felt like this value was no longer a value in the banking culture. My values give me a sense of purpose and help me to see what suits me best.

   Recognition of your own core values may come to you naturally, or the process can be a struggle. I wish I could say that I knew from a young age what I valued in life and what I wanted to do with my career. It took many years and multiple jobs within the bank for me to understand myself, my values and the importance of keeping those things in alignment with the work I did. For me, I think the answer was there for a long time, but I just didn't see it. I must have been looking for a dramatic event to make things clear. There was no earthquake that produced a sign saying, 'This way is your personal path to career happiness!' In hindsight, understanding my values shouldn't have been such a mystery.

"You just decide what your values are in life and what you are going to do, and then you feel like you count, and that makes life worth living. It makes my life meaningful."

- *Annie Lennox*

Questions I ask clients to help them discover their values and strengths are: Who do you admire? What qualities do they possess? What skills do they have?

I invite you to take this opportunity now think of someone you admire and write down the qualities you most admire in them. It can be someone you know personally or someone you look up to.

1. ______________________________________

2. ______________________________________

3. ____

4. ____

5. ____

When you find out what you value and when you work on your personal growth you will understand *why* you do what you do and how you can make changes to create the life you want. Your understanding and perception of yourself and the world around you can determine the decisions you make and the direction you take in life. I found that even early experiences can shape our lives.

I was born in Co. Louth, the eldest of four children into a very happy home. One of my earliest memories was being in hospital and my mother coming in with one white knee-length sock to take me home. I had a hip operation when I was two, as I was born with "click hip". I didn't walk until I was three years old. Being born the eldest of four sometimes felt as though I had to be the responsible one.

I was young going to school, I just turned four and as a result I repeated sixth class all my friends had gone onto secondary school, I felt I wasn't good enough to go to secondary school. I know at the time my parents were only doing what was best for me.

I remember going into secondary school to sit the entrance exam, feeling that I was not good enough, feeling like I was going to fail the exam. I was terrified. In secondary school, I had friends and I had some good fun, but I always felt a sense of isolation, and having been bullied, this just compounded it. I was very shy and not very confident. On one occasion when I was in sixth year some friends were sitting around the kitchen table and they shared that I should "come out of my shell."

I found it hard to communicate, I was afraid to speak up, afraid of being judged and afraid of what other people would think. One of the greatest lessons I have learned is, "what other people think of you, is none of your business". What other people feel, think, say or do is one hundred percent about them. What you feel, think, say or do, belongs to you one hundred percent.

I was afraid in school. I was afraid of boys! I was afraid of not having enough. Looking back now fear is what drove me and kept moving me forward to the next level in work, to drive me to keep getting that promotion!

Understanding my feelings helped me to communicate better with others and helped me to understand myself more. Feelings are part of everyday life and are interspersed with just about everything we do. I am not my feelings, they are not who I am, they merely represent who I am in the moment that I feel them.

Being unable to express feelings growing up and not being able to communicate to others in my family and school how I was feeling, caused blocks in my relationships and possibly led to my poor self-esteem growing up. I now know that it is essential for me to acknowledge my feelings and to be aware of them.

The feeling of anxiety and the feeling of excitement manifest the same feelings in the body e.g. goose bumps, butterflies in your tummy and sweaty palms. For example. when I tried abseiling, I had to keep telling myself how excited I was even though I was petrified.

I always felt not good enough growing up, I'm never going to achieve anything and guess what, it was a self-fulfilling fallacy!

My leaving cert is one example, which was mediocre. I believed I couldn't achieve anything, so I didn't study enough, and I got results to show it. There is no blame though because I now know that if I want to change a negative feeling, I have first to change the way I think about it and what I am feeling bad about. What do you believe about yourself or what stories are you telling yourself? 'I can't go for that promotion, I'm not good enough, I can't start my own business' etc. I find writing things down helps.

Journaling is a great way to acknowledge how you are feeling. Instead of free-writing I answer questions.

How do I want to feel today?

____

What are my intentions today?

____

What do I want to receive today?

____

What do I want to give today?

____

"The Key to Feeling good is to decide to stop Feeling bad"

- *Gabby Bernstein.*

My motivations have now changed. I still have fears, a fear of financial security and not having enough to pay the bills every month, but I am working on this every day and trusting more and more that it will all work out.

Changing my mindset from a fixed mindset to a growth mindset was not easy and didn't happen overnight. Changing my negative belief pattern of "not being good enough" and having the feeling like everything would fail took time. I still work on it. Thinking is one the greatest powers we possess, and it's our choice to use it negatively or positively. All beliefs are a choice and choices can be changed. I don't allow the voice of my fears to be louder than the other voices in my head; thoughts are very powerful, and I try to make them positive. I choose positivity now.

As part of my morning routine and before I even step out of bed, I firstly acknowledge at least 10 things I am grateful for in life and then I make an intention for the day ahead. This morning routine really helps me to create a positive state of mind.

"Gratitude is the healthiest of all human emotions. The more you express gratitude for what you have, the more likely you will have even more to express gratitude for."

- *Zig Ziglar*

Learn to have trust in yourself and trust your instinct, it rarely steers you in the wrong direction. It is your inner compass! Looking and listening eventually helped me to find my purpose in life. Go with your gut feeling.

The heart is a powerful communicator to the brain and the stomach, and this is verified by science and biology. There is a very real reason we keep hearing the advice, "listen to your heart." I believe that there are signs everywhere, but if we look at the word **heart**, within it are the words **ear** and **hear**.

It's telling you everything you need to know. Whatever journey you're on, whatever your purpose may be, it's valuable to know your heart is a trusted informant. Trust your heart. The heart is in a constant flow of communication to the brain and it actually sends larger volumes of information to the brain than the brain sends to the heart. The heart has its own central nervous system, and the heart, brain, and stomach are made of neural tissue and those three are all connected. We must take responsibility for our life. The response that creates our experiences of life comes from ourselves.

When you change your thinking, you change your beliefs.

Change begins with your mind. Beliefs are nothing more than a by-product of what you have thought about long enough,

something that you have bought into. What you believe, what you think, is a collection of continual thoughts that have formed themselves into a conviction. When you break down the process of thinking into a manageable number of steps, you reduce the perceived risk associated with change.

When you change your beliefs, you change your expectations.

Belief is the knowledge that we can do something. It is the inner feeling that what we undertake, we can accomplish. For the most part, all of us have the ability to look at something and know whether we can do it or not. Our beliefs control everything we do. If we believe we can or we believe we cannot, we are correct.

When you change your expectations, you change your attitude.

Your expectations are going to determine your attitude. Most people get used to average; they get used to second best. Nelson Boswell said, "The first and most important step toward success is the expectation that we can succeed."

When you change your attitude, you change your behaviour.

When our attitude begins to change, when we become involved with something, our behaviour begins to change.

When you change your behaviour, you change your performance.

People would rather live with old problems than new solutions. We would rather be comfortable than correct. We would rather stay in a routine than make changes. Even when we know that the changes are going to be better for us, we often don't make them because we feel uncomfortable or awkward about making that kind of a change. Until we get courage and get used to living with something that is not comfortable, we cannot get any better.

When you change your performance, you change your life.

A person can fail, turn around and understand their failure to make it a success. A person who makes excuses for everything will never truly succeed. Don't you know some people who just have an excuse for everything? Why they could not, should not, did not, would not, have not, will not. When you excuse what you are doing and excuse where you are, and you allow the exceptions, you fail to reach your potential. It is impossible to turn excuses into possibilities.

What makes you happy?

If you don't know what makes you happy, here's something I found useful to do. I wrote down a list of twenty things that I enjoy or that I had enjoyed doing when I was a child and growing up. What interests did you have growing up? Baking, football, did you enjoy putting on shows for others, singing, dancing? When I was doing this exercise, I completely forgot about things I enjoyed during my childhood. For me it was playing tennis. I used to play tennis when I was a child, the only sport I played growing up. I got lessons every week from the local coach, this was rural village in early 80's, so we were lucky to have a tennis coach living in the village. Over thirty years later I'm now back playing, not so good, but it is great fun and with a great group of local people. A new tennis club has been formed in the past year and so many people are getting great enjoyment from it. One of things that brings me most joy in my life is spending time with my son, whom I am very proud of.

Now take your top five things and see if there something that you could do in the evening and weekends which you would find enjoyable.

It's important to take responsibility for your life happiness. Remember that you are not your circumstances or story, you are you and you can create the life that works for you! You have everything you need to do it, just remember who you are. Start thinking in terms of abundance and success. How do you talk to yourself? Is it positive or negative? When you say the words, I AM, what do you usually put after it? If it's not positive and powerful, change it! Self-talk can determine your happiness. And the words I AM are two of the most powerful words in English language. Be careful how you use them!

"Twenty years from now you will be more disappointed by the things that you didn't do than by the ones you did do."

— Mark Twain

As a result of changing my mindset I have been able to do so many things that perhaps I wouldn't have, had I not focused on personal growth. I learned to create a life that gives me meaning and purpose, and now I support individuals and businesses to clarify and realise their personal and business ambitions. In January 2019 I established Anu Change www.anuchange.com and I have been focused on helping people be the best they can be ever since! It is my passion to bring the best out in people. We all have potential that if tapped into can make amazing things happen!

Be the Best You Can Be

by Emma Hill

Growing up I was always competitive. I played a lot of sport; hockey, swimming, gymnastics (to name a few) and I distinctly remember the writing on the gym wall, at 8 years old, when I was doing my 150th sit-up, 'There's no such thing as second place' and 'No pain, no gain'. Now, I can image that these slogans may sound a little harsh, but along with my parents who had their own slogan "You can be anything you want to be", they became quite a powerful mantra.

I think at this stage I need to point out that I am not the most talented person you will ever meet, or the prettiest or the most intelligent. This is not about being the best. It's about being your best. There will always be someone who seems more successful, more content, more together, but that's not you. If you never settle for anything other than your best, then you will always know in your heart that you have achieved everything you could.

Being able to identify what your best life looks like is the first step, you always need to have a goal. Sometimes those goals are small and can be as simple as eating more healthily or making sure you speak to your best friend on the phone more often. And sometimes they are the ultimate goals of being rich and famous or a mother or father. Close your eyes and imagine what you want your life to be like. Put yourself there, see yourself slimmer, relaxing with family and friends, receiving that business award. Whatever it is, you need to know where you are going, to be able to get there.

I grew up in Manchester, I have a Pharmacology degree from Newcastle University and am currently the Director of three Bird of Prey companies in West Wales. Erm okay, was this where I saw myself ten years ago?! No, not at all. Did I know that I wanted to run my own company back then? Still, probably not. I always remember when people asked us in class "What do you want to be when you grow up?" my friends all seemed to know; nurse, fireman, footballer, and I would always think, 'I haven't got a clue!'. But there is something I've always known; I want to be successful.

For some people it's money, for others it's security, whatever the driver to your goal, embrace it. Then give it 100%. If you do this then you will always know you did your best to make it happen. It's not surprising that most of the time you will achieve it. There is nothing worse than thinking I could have done better.

Once you identify what your best life looks like, recognising why you are driven to do what you are doing is key, without this understanding it is very easy to be blown off track or just give up altogether. My 'why' started out very personal, I wanted to continue my relationship but along with that it gave me an opportunity of a new challenge and chance to live an even better life.

I had always wanted to travel and see the world. In 2010 I had just met my partner Alex and we both decided this would be a good time to take time off and fulfil this dream. I was lucky enough to get a sabbatical from my role as a Business Manager in a top pharmaceutical company and we headed off around the world for a year. Wanting to make it the best trip ever (obviously!) we travelled around twenty-two countries in twelve months, covering most of South America, Japan, China and South East Asia, finishing in Australia and New Zealand.

It was about two months into our trip, and we had crossed the border; on one of our smoother South American crossings, into Brazil and were heading for Iguacu Falls. Having previously been to Canada I was expecting something similar, but this makes Niagara look like a leaky tap! It's so overwhelming to stand there and experience, you can't help but feel the power of nature, and it goes on and on. To top it off, next to the falls is Parque das Aves, a Brazilian Bird Park. We proceeded to spend the next two hours staring at a pair of Harpy eagles willing them to move! For those of you that are not bird geeks, the Harpy eagle is one of the most elaborate looking raptor species and claims to be the most powerful in the world. Their diet consists predominantly of monkeys and sloths and they are only found in very small numbers in this part of the world. So, having watched David Attenborough obsessively growing up, this was a once in a lifetime opportunity. Like most well fed birds of prey though, after a couple of hours, we had to concede that they were not going to start flying around and were content to just sit and be stared at. Still, it was incredible. It was at this point Alex turned to me and said three words that were to change my life as I knew it 'I miss Mally.'

Maleki is a male Harris Hawk that Alex got as a chick in 2004. Originally the plan was to hunt with him as a hobby but when he was made redundant a few years later it became a business opportunity. At the time when we met, he was doing a few experience days and giving people the chance to fly Mally themselves, but things hadn't really taken off and he was getting a bit disheartened with it all. So, when I suggested going away for a year, he was keen to join me. Mally would remain at home to be looked after by his parents. They also gained my two cats at the same time; where would we be without parents? Anyway, at the time of our travels we were unclear as to what our future together looked like. We had only been together, long distance, for a year and where we would live when we returned to the UK was still up for debate. "So, we are going back to Wales then?"

was my response, which was met with a wry smile. Newcastle city centre living is not conducive to a bird of prey business.

We spent the next few months visiting numerous zoos and bird centres around the world and in the evenings over dinner we started to develop a plan. The goal was to own the best bird of prey centre in the UK, and put on the best shows, so people would come and visit us from all over the world, instead of anywhere else.

We all make excuses for why we don't do things, but if you don't try then you can never succeed. Only you can make things happen. Once you realise your goal and why you want to achieve it, you must ask yourself why haven't you done it already? I've got no time, it's too much effort, it costs too much money. These are all just excuses. If you want to be the best, you must do your best. As a child we throw ourselves into new situations all the time, it's only as we get older, we get so cautious, we imagine obstacles that aren't really there.

When I decided I was going to give up my well paid, secure job, it was a bit frightening. I drove a nice company car, had private healthcare and a lovely bonus scheme. Being guaranteed an income every month I knew exactly what I could afford and that I'd get my pay cheque on the same day, like clockwork. Leaving all of this behind and not knowing how much I would earn each month was scary. My family were even more nervous, they reminded me how much I had worked for so far to get to where I was and some really tried to talk me out of it. When you decide to make a big change in your life, everyone will have an opinion. Some will be supportive, and others won't be. Try not to take on all their fears when deciding whether to go ahead or not.

I drove a nice company car, but it wasn't my dream car and had a lovely bonus scheme, but it wasn't giving me hundreds of thousands of pounds each year. I had a guaranteed income every month, but I had limited earning potential. I knew exactly what I could afford but I couldn't afford all the things I dreamt of. For me to have my best life I needed to make a change.

Fear of failure is a very real emotion and always a possibility when you try something new. But what if you never take the risk and never realise your full potential. Which is more bearable?

I always find the best way to decide if something is worth doing is to imagine the best and the worst-case scenario. If I give up my career and our bird of prey centre plan fails, then what? I get another job. But if I give up my career and our bird of prey centre plan succeeds, I get to create an amazing business that is enjoyed by many people and I get to be super successful and live my best life. Trust me, it's not going to be easy. Nothing worth doing ever is. You need to weigh up if it is worth all the stress and strain and all the things you have to give up. Remember 'no pain, no gain'.

When we began our journey and I was still earning my nice wages and bonuses. We tried our best to save as much as we could, knowing the next few years would be tight. Once I gave up my job, we had to make sacrifices to the lifestyle we were used to. We downgraded our beautiful home to a rental flat with single glazing and no central heating and when things were really bad, we moved in with Alex's parents. We drove our work van as our only vehicle and had to forego seeing friends and family on special occasions as we just couldn't afford the travel or the time.

Over the last eight years I've lost friends due to us focusing on making our life successful. I moved four hundred miles to follow my dream. Along with having a reduced income, as is usual when starting a new business, I also work with animals. They need to be fed and looked after daily. That includes Christmas Day and days when we are sick, or it snows. Not everyone will understand what it takes to reach your goal and when you can't drop things and be there for them as you were before, those people may not understand. It's not been easy to accept this, and I've had many times where I have been devastated to not make a significant event. Each time you must weigh up the pros and cons and decide if your goal is worth the loss.

On the other hand, my good friends are scattered around the world and they understand what it takes to do what we do and are proud of what we have achieved. It is their support and recognition that keeps me motivated. Watching my nieces and nephews when they visit our centres and experience what we have created makes it all worthwhile.

Whilst the journey can be difficult along the way you meet new and amazing people and learn so many new things. So, when you have those days where is all feels like it's going wrong and you are wondering if it's still worth it, look back and realise just how far you have come and what you stand to gain when you achieve your vision. To do this, it's important to understand where you started from.

Acknowledging where you are when you start out is imperative. If you have never run a metre in your life, then expecting to be able to run a marathon in a week is unrealistic. But by knowing where you are now and where you want to be, you can start to create a clear vision and a step by step process to help you achieve your dreams. No matter where you want to get to, there must be a beginning. If the goal seems too big to be realistic, remember you have to start somewhere, and you can achieve anything.

How do you turn one Harris Hawk into the best Bird of Prey Centre in the UK?

In the beginning we had nothing but a hawk and the basis for an experience day company, that was built on the ethos of making sure birds were given the opportunity to fly regularly and well, that was it. I suppose if we had a surplus of cash we could have gone out and bought a piece of land and paid for it to have happened over night, but neither of us really knew the first thing about running a bird of prey centre back then, so we took a step by step approach. I agreed to us moving back to Wales after our trip was over and offered to support us to give Alex the opportunity to develop towards our goal. Once the business was big enough to sustain us both, I would give up my job and join him.

I look back now and we had a basis of a plan but if I'm honest it was vague and maybe if we'd have been more specific, we could have achieved things sooner. As with most things in life once you get into something it is all consuming and difficult to see where to go next, so you just keep driving on.

In June 2019 I got an invite to a Women's Business Conference to celebrate female entrepreneurship. I had just been told I had a month to move my Owl Centre and I was in a bit of a mess, so I decided a day out of the office and a bit of motivation was exactly what was required. That's where I met Donna. She was one of the speakers at the event and her words and the opportunity she posed was just what I needed.

Have a plan and break it down in to manageable steps was one of her many pearls of wisdom. I have a habit of wanting everything done yesterday and with so many plates spinning trying to run a new start-up and now needing to move and reopen an owl centre, focus and a clear plan was so important for my sanity. I needed to take a step back and visualise what success looked like now things were different, then break it down in to a step by step approach to achieve it. The most pertinent bit of advice was to assign timeframes to my goals. Not only does this make it manageable, it helps to keep you on the most effective track.

Imagine your goal, you are there living it, write it down, make it real. Then work out what you will do in the next week towards that goal, the next month and the next 6 months. By breaking it down into bite sized pieces the task doesn't seem quite so overwhelming anymore.

Success for me is my businesses running smoothly and being recognised as two of the best tourist attractions in the UK. What would this mean to me personally? I would have a supportive team around me that are all working towards that same goal, giving me and Alex the time to have weekends away with family and friends and holidays. By having a clear step by step process that includes the actions I need to take and by when, I can see exactly how I am going to achieve this.

Now you have a plan, the next step is to implement it. To achieve anything takes time and effort. For the first five years we were giving 100% all the time and it was gruelling. We were living in a dingy flat with no central heating and we were working every day. We weren't big enough to employ another falconer and because we were working with animals and up to 30 birds by now, they always needed looking after. Every penny we had was put back into growing and developing. At this point we'd already come so far and achieved so much. All it would take would be to find a venue and open a centre and all of it would be worth it.

Over the first year Pembrokeshire Falconry became very popular. Alex was out with guests daily and at the weekends I would join him too. We were starting to make a name for ourselves, but things weren't moving quickly enough. The goal was to open a bird of prey centre and to do that we needed a venue. The only venues who knew who we were, were the ones we did our private experiences with. We needed to expand and create a flying display team, so we could showcase our skills to a wider audience. By the summer of 2015 we had a top-class display team and provided over 120 flying displays across fifteen different venues in six weeks. We had five regular locations we displayed at and our shows were consistently increasing visitor numbers for the attractions.

Due to our ongoing success and recognition, in 2016 we finally signed the contracts to open The Secret Owl Garden, the largest owl centre in Wales, at the venue where we had been doing our experiences since we started. As the saying goes "it never rains but it pours", a month later we were approached by The National Botanic Garden of Wales asking if we would consider partnering with them too. They are a major tourist attraction in Wales and have a great ethos of Education and Conservation which fits nicely with our own. This was the opportunity we had been looking for since 2011 so naturally we jumped at the chance to design our own centre from scratch. In the space of three months we'd gone from no bird of prey centres to two.

2016 was a massive year for us, we were the choice provider of all the bird of prey displays across West Wales, we had built fantastic relationships with large, influential attractions and we were starting to be recognised for the high-quality business we had created. We were number one on TripAdvisor in the County, we won a Countryside Alliance Rural Oscar, were named the Best Experience in Pembrokeshire and appeared on many television shows, including The One Show. All the hard work, effort and sleepless nights we had put into getting here was starting to pay off.

I don't think there is ever a point where you don't have to do everything to the best of your ability if you want to be successful. At this point we couldn't sit back and take our foot off the gas, instead the addition of staff and partnerships with two very different organisations added their own complexities. Each day brings a new challenge and within those challenges I continue to ask myself 'what is the goal, why do I want to achieve it and is it worth it?', for me, that answer continues to be yes.

On reflection, did we bite off more than we could chew? Maybe. Throughout my journey I am always learning and one thing I had never considered was that not every opportunity is the right opportunity. Giving 100% to the wrong thing can be as detrimental as not putting enough effort in. Making sure the plan is the right plan and focusing on the things that will make the biggest difference to achieving your goal is key. Will I be any more successful having two bird of prey centres or would I be more productive spending my time focussing on one?

Giving 100% all the time is exhausting. You need to find ways to relax and take time away from it all. One of the biggest things I have learned recently (and I am still trying to work on) is that giving 100% doesn't need to mean 100% all the time. Over the years our business has been all consuming and when you are driven to succeed it can be difficult to focus on anything else. I have spent many a time wide awake in the middle of the night because my brain can't switch off. I have recently made a concerted effort to find other things to do that can take me away from thinking and talking about our business all the time. Whilst it is important to give 100% whilst you are there, too much time focusing on work and not you can make you ill. Learning to not feel guilty for taking a day off or a couple of hours to have my hair or nails done, has been a challenge. But I have found that this time makes me more productive. Putting my laptop down in the evening and going for a run or watching a film helps me to sleep better and the following day I achieve more.

When you work so hard to achieve something over a long period of time, staying motivated when things don't quite go to plan is a challenge. Many times, over the last few years, it would have been easier to give up and go and get a job with a good salary and less stress, but that would have meant giving up on my best life.

I look back now and realise that in the middle of all of this we didn't really stop and enjoy the moment. Of course, on the night of the awards we celebrated the wins. We used it as a marketing opportunity to let people know that we were the best and had a nice meal and a few drinks. But I never really believed it. Because it wasn't the endgame, I sort of skipped over what it had taken to get us to this point in the first place. The 'big' goal overshadowed every success we had along the way and I forgot how much we had achieved to be where we were.

It's really important that as part of the plan you make and the steps you take, to achieve your best life, that you take time to reflect on how far you have come. Staying motivated is difficult when it feels like everything is against you or when things are not moving at the pace you want them to. By acknowledging all the milestones along the way and taking the time to really give yourself the credit for what you've achieved, you will feel happier and inspired to continue your journey. It especially comes in handy when things don't work out quite the way you want them to.

The Secret Owl Garden opened in 2017 and the following June we opened The British Bird of Prey Centre. Whilst we managed to achieve major milestones, welcoming over 20,000 people a year and being the number one attraction in Pembrokeshire on TripAdvisor, things were not going well with The Secret Owl Garden. The venue we'd opened in didn't have the same ambition we had. We hoped they'd embrace the high-quality attraction we'd created and want it to be as successful as we did, this wasn't to be the case. Realising it was going to be unsustainable to stay we had to make the difficult decision to relocate and start again from the beginning.

We went through every range of emotions and ups and downs, questioning everything we should or could have done differently. Our first centre and it was a failure, how could we have let this happen? After the initial shock of learning we had such a short time frame to move, we came up with a plan, found a new venue and moved our owls to a new site and continued to trade two weeks later. Don't get me wrong, this was a traumatic time but the point I'm trying to make is don't give up. When things go wrong, and they inevitably will one day, you have a choice; give up or keep fighting.

We have now spent the last few months reflecting on all of what we did well and what we would like to improve the second time around. We have the luxury of hindsight. We won't make the same mistakes again and our new Secret Owl Garden will be bigger and better than before.

During this time, The British Bird of Prey Centre has been incredibly successful already. Having been shortlisted for many awards, made numerous television and radio appearances and been visited by eminent people like Prince Charles. All the things we learned along the way are helping us. We made the decision to take the issues we've faced as feedback rather than failure and use them to our advantage.

Make sure you surround yourself with the best people that have the same drive and ambition as you do and keep going. Each time something knocks you back learn from it and get up tougher than before. What doesn't kill you will only make you stronger.

I've found the most difficult part of running a company is feeling alone. 'It's lonely at the top' as the cliché goes. It was interesting having a conversation with my Dad recently, who could relate to this, having run his own company for fifty years. He told me people still treat him differently now. Finding teams to support you is the key to success and then finding your place in those teams, is just as significant. I can't emphasize how important it is to have the right people around you, bad attitudes can break your spirit very quickly.

I am lucky to have been able to share my journey with my husband, we are a good team, but we know we cannot do it all on our own like we did in the first few years. Back then it was our families who supported us on our crazy journey. They helped us buy birds we needed, made us sandwiches and dinner when we didn't have time to eat and listened to our endless stories about what we were up to next. When the Secret Owl Garden needed to move quickly, we were humbled by the number of people who went out of their way to turn up and lift, carry and help us to move. It was their support which kept me sane during all the stress and I don't think I'll ever be able to convey my gratitude to them all.

We now have a great team working at The British Bird of Prey Centre and with their drive and enthusiasm we have developed a centre that we are proud of. Each of them and the many volunteers that support us day in and day out strive for that goal of being the best. Alex and I are starting to be able to take some time to live our lives and enjoy our personal time together too and that is invaluable. Everyone needs support and I am very grateful to everyone that has helped me along the way.

When I look back, I can picture the people who played the biggest parts in making me who I am and getting me where I want to be. Some of these people have been there throughout; family and life-long friends. Some I have met only for a day and others are recent additions to my life, like the Welsh girls writing this book. I have, and continue to, learn from them every day.

In business, having a coach or a mentor was something I never thought I'd be interested in, but it turns out that having a fresh pair of eyes looking through things has helped me to channel my energy more efficiently. Having someone to talk to throughout all the changes that have happened this year has definitely made me a better businesswoman and a saner person! At times when I have been stressed and unable to focus, having someone to go through things with has meant I've made better decisions that have kept me on the path to achieving my goals.

No one climbs a mountain alone. Asking for and accepting support doesn't take anything away from your achievements. It's ok to need help to be the best you can be. It's just not possible to be strong enough all the time to be successful on your own. Having a team to share your success with, people to motivate you when you are feeling down and those you can give support and advice to in return, is guaranteed to make you a better you.

Into the Light

by Shelly Maher

Saturday 1st of September 2007 was the day I took my last drink. I remember it well. I felt as low as a snake's belly and my head felt like a washing machine on fast spin. I was sick of being sick. I didn't know if I was coming or going, and I felt Insecure and shameful, not remembering my behavior or what I had said to my loved ones the night before — making empty promises that I wouldn't come home drunk had to stop. I couldn't do it anymore. Even though I had tried all sorts of things to stop drinking, changing my usual spirit drinks to beer, drinking slowly, drinking a pint of water in between drinks, even going out at different times, I didn't seem to be able to stop. I wanted to stop but I couldn't do it on my own. I didn't know how to change, but something had to change. I needed to get outside help.

I had two choices, which were to get busy living or get busy dying. Half measures wouldn't work anymore. It had gone too far. I needed real help. And if I was to get better, that meant removing my ego and getting out of my own way. In desperation, I picked up my phone and called my brother, Patrick, that Saturday morning. I asked him if he would bring me to an AA meeting. I thought maybe they might help. He agreed but only under one condition, that I wouldn't take any drink for the next three days.

That was one of the worst times of my life. I was full of fear and I stayed in bed the whole weekend. I didn't trust myself not to drink. It was the longest three days of my life, waiting for that Monday evening to come around. I would have gone to any lengths not to pick up that first drink, waiting for that meeting to come around. I remember lying in my bed sweating, sobbing into my pillow. I just couldn't believe that my life had gone down such a bad spiral. I was so out of control. I was afraid to get dressed or have a shower; I didn't trust myself not to drink. I kept telling myself that I had to stay at home until Monday. Dear reader, the one thing you must understand about Alcoholism is that it is very cunning and baffling. It would just take a second (before I would even know it) to have either planned my next drink or have one in my hand, wondering to myself how the hell that happened again. The one thing I was sure of was that I was desperately unwell, lost and confused. I had hit my rock bottom. I was a shattered broken woman.

As I walked into my first AA meeting, I didn't know what to expect. The meeting started on time and I remember thinking to myself, 'This is a strange bunch of people. They seem to be happy and at ease even, dare I say it. They seemed glad to be here.' They made me feel very welcome and asked me if I would like a coffee. I remember thinking, 'None of these people look like Alcoholics.'

I took my seat and listened. They went around one by one talking about their day and how it went. It was coming closer to my turn to speak and I was beginning to get very anxious, I didn't know what I was going to say. My hands were getting very sweaty. My heart was pumping out of my chest. Then it was my turn to say, 'Hi, my name is Shelly and I'm an alcoholic.' Well, one thing I wasn't going to admit was that I was an alcoholic! Of course, at that time I was still in denial. I felt I had nothing in common with that room of strangers and I certainly wasn't going to say I was one of them! I had no understanding of alcoholism. I didn't even understand what it was, at the time. Then a voice out of nowhere asked if I would like to say something. I declined, hoping that they would go to the next person quickly, but the same person went on to say, 'It's grand, no pressure, it was lovely to meet you and you are very welcome.' She said that I was the most important person in the room that evening, and if I think I had a drink problem, I was in the right place, all I needed to do was give it a chance for ninety days. That meant going back, and that didn't appeal to me one bit. But I knew I had to do something to get better. Reluctantly, and after a lot of thinking, I decided to go back to the meetings. In fact, I did ninety meetings in ninety days and, as the days fell into weeks and months the fog began to lift. Little by little I was finding out about myself and who I was.

It brought me to places that I wouldn't have gone in my wildest dreams, had I not attended the meetings. I began the ninety days helpless and hopeless. I was five stone overweight for my height, I was horribly malnourished, I was in chronic fatigue to the point of exhaustion and I was in a debilitating depression. But after the ninety days I was literally a different person. My thinking became clearer, even my skin became clearer. I desperately wanted this to work, so I kept going back. I could see the difference in my kids' faces, trust was being built up again and it felt good. I was becoming the mom I wanted to be and the wife I wanted to be. I just wanted to be happy and healthy and to be there for the people I loved. Something inside me was giving me the strength I was searching for and I began believing in myself again.

I decided to continue the process a day at a time. For the first nine months I just listened. I never opened my mouth. I was too fragile, too numb, but I knew that it was working. I did not want to drink anymore. I wanted my life back. Going to meetings on a regular basis helped. My obsession for alcohol lifted. Truth be told, AA got a hold of me, I didn't get a hold of AA for some time.

Since reaching out and asking for help, four years passed and my life became manageable, sometimes quickly and sometimes slowly, but then I hit another rock bottom, which was my sobriety. Although my thinking had become clearer, and I had become stronger, the residual pain of my behavior in drunken stupor was still very real. I had developed the tools to deal with life on life's terms, but at that time my marriage had fallen apart and both my children had decided to stay with their dad in the family home. It hurt like hell, but I had to respect their choice. I left the family home and I moved to a different town. This is where I met J.

I continued going to meetings on a regular basis for six months and I did a full-time course, which kept me very busy, but I knew I had to make more changes. If I was going to make progress, I had to get a sponsor for ongoing support. I knew there had to be more to life than just managing life. I wanted the fun-loving Shelly back. This is where the real work began!

I needed someone strong to help me on the next step moving forward, and having watched and listened to J, and having seen what a good program she had, I wanted what she had. For the first time in years I reached out and asked for help again. I remember being so nervous because I was afraid of being rejected. That wasn't to be the case. It was a Tuesday when I approached J to ask her to be my sponsor. She said that she would think about it and thanked me for asking her. She told me that if I was serious about it, she would meet me for coffee on Friday after the meeting. These were the rules. There are not many rules, but this was the only way it was going to work — to be accountable for my time management and respect of her time. It was lovely that she gave up her private time and her home for me, a safe place, so we could work together.

I had to knuckle down, open the big book, read it, understand it, and then apply it. There were little hitches along the way, but I just figured them out by using the Step 4 list, which is, *Pray, write, talk, pray.* Pray around it, write it down, talk about it with my sponsor, and pray again for gratitude. With that step I was able to verbalize what I needed to say, which helped me immensely in my recovery. Being aware, clever and smart, I knew what was going on and what I needed to change. I hated the world, I hated anyone that had kids, I MISSED my kids! I was full of "poor me" self-pity, even though I was sober. I had been sober for four years at that point and I was acting like a dry drunk. I knew I had to change my attitude. Glancing back at it now years later, I was aware of my behavior I just wasn't being accountable for my behavior. So, J got down to business very quickly indeed.

I started working the program, despite how I was feeling, putting it into my daily living and taking responsibility for my own behavior. I worked through the twelve steps with J. It took me a full year to accomplish a good understanding of this very simple program. Once again, the fog slowly lifted, I had a different outlook on life, I felt stronger than before. Despite moving, family issues and everything going on in my life with my children, I was able to cope with it immensely well, unbelievably well actually. I learned great thinking, and my mantra "In with the light, out with the shite" helped too! Doing this also helped me to be more tolerant towards others. I started thinking before I spoke, I became kinder to myself and wasn't so self-critical. I stopped being a people-pleaser, so I didn't get overwhelmed. Saying no to people was the hardest task after that. The first no was the hardest, but it got easier with time. This helped me to not get so overwhelmed and gave me a choice to make clear and precise decisions, making for the greater good of everyone involved.

I did plenty of meditation, which moved me forward very quickly and solidly. Meditation has been a huge part of my life from a very early age. In the darkest hours in my life I always found the light, through breath. It helped me relax. Getting through being dyslexic in Ireland in the early 80's was difficult. It was not a good place for any child to have dyslexia. I'm so pleased for the younger generation today that they are given the support that they need for our education system. Growing up I always felt lonely, even in a room full of people. I was fun-loving, caring, popular and friendly. I had lots of friends, but I always felt inadequate. I guess what I'm trying to say is that my wiring was off early on in life so when I came of age, drinking ended up being my best friend.

There is a saying in AA — "It is much easier to STAY clean and sober than it is to GET clean and sober." If you are of the addictive type, it's like your entire life addiction is a dis-ease of disorder of the personality, the spirit of the mind, and eventually the body and social life. It attacks all fronts of one's life. It affected my life, even before I found my drug of choice (alcohol) and before that it was anything that felt good. Once I learned a new way, I adjusted and finally I was able to stay away from it. In recovery, one day at a time, with the help of my sponsor and home group, made it easier to stay sober than trying to do it alone. In my experience alcohol addiction was a progressive illness and as the years went by and it got worse, the consequences got worse too. There are three options if you are addicted, which are (a) lock up, (b) cover up with dirt, or (c) sober up. The ultimate outcome is jails, institutions and death, if you stay on that addiction path.

I was a mess for two decades but, and this may sound crazy, I would not change a single day; it has made me become the person I am today. I now have peace with my past. These past twelve years have been some of the greatest of my life and my days keep getting better and better.

The Promises of AA

If we are painstaking about this phase of our development, we will be amazed before we are halfway through. We will not regret the past nor wish to shut the door on it. We will comprehend the word serenity and we will know peace. No matter how far down the scale we have gone, we will see how our experiences can benefit others. That feeling of uselessness and self-pity will disappear. We will lose interest in selfish things and gain interest in our fellows. Self-seeking will slip away. Our whole attitude and outlook upon life will change. Fear of people and of economic insecurity will leave us. We will intuitively know how to handle situations which used to baffle us. We will suddenly realize what a God (of your understanding) is doing for us but we could not do for ourselves. Are these extravagant promises? We think not. They are being fulfilled among us sometimes quickly sometimes slowly. They will always materialize if we work for them. it works if you work it. Keep coming back."

I have a higher power in my life today, a higher power of my understanding (Universe) which helps me. I can say to myself that energy goes where energy flows, and I direct it toward what is good for me. I embrace change today. Implementing the twelve-step program on my own journey and helping and supporting others along the way with my *Gratitude with Attitude* outlook on life. I feel truly blessed. Now I keep it simple. The moment I wake up before my feet touch the ground, I take three deep breaths and say, 'Thank you, thank you, thank you. Good morning higher power, how may I serve you today? Let me do your work through my hands. I am enough and so it is.' It's a small but very effective prayer that works for me. My higher power has a great sense of humor too...well let's put it like this, the fun-loving Shelly is back! I'm smiling to myself even now, knowing that people trust me again and I feel alive for me and my loved ones.

Implementing Step 9 of AA has helped with family members and friends. Step 9 is "Make direct amends to such people wherever possible, except when to do so would injure them or others." I have made good progress in this area, and whilst I am aware there are many roads to go, I am focused on making continual progress.

Only recently, I was driving a car with some of my family up Mount Teide, an active Volcano on the Island of Tenerife, with its windy roads and amazing scenery. The next day we went to the most picturesque village in Tenerife called Masca. We also skied a few times during the holiday, and I experienced my first love (sailing) with the people who are dear to me. We shared a wonderful experience with dolphins and whales and, being Aquarius, I felt very calm, focused and connected. I receive the most creative downloads with ease and clarity in, on or around water.

I am so very grateful for the life I have today. It is beyond my wildest dreams, especially considering how I used to be. I can look at myself in the mirror now and love the person who is there. I LOVE myself from the inside out. I feel huge gratitude to the AA members I have met on my travels from America and Australia and all the beautiful countries in between, and my home group and sponsor, for without them I may not be here. I am especially grateful to my family: Paddy, Bronagh, Tom, Caoimhe and Emmet for all their loving support, and a special mention to R & M (thinking of you always).

I now understand that there is nothing on this beautiful planet of ours that I can't handle on any given day. I feel so free and confident in my thinking and I believe in myself. I am Shelly. I am back. I'm living my dream life and every day in every way my life gets better and better!

Stop and Listen
Life Might be Teaching You Something

by Lisa Mooney

"In order to love who you are,

you cannot hate the experiences that shaped you."

I am Lisa, a 50-something singleton, again, and I believe that you can achieve anything you set your mind to if you believe you can. A famous Henry Ford quote, *"Whether you think you can, or you think you can't – you're right,"* emphasizes how much attitude determines success or failure. It's just a matter of listening and learning, again and again if necessary!

I've experienced many things in life, divorced twice, mother of two (now adult) wonderful children, a homemaker, carer of my elderly mother with health issues, small business owner, dance fitness instructor, office administrator, freelance writer, a world champion line-dancer (I should be more proud of that!), traveller, runner, walker, cyclist, swimmer, hiker, trekker and... Oh yeah, and a survivor!

Life is short, you need to do or find what makes you happy, what brings you joy. Sometimes that can be hard to do; there's always going to be obstacles to get around and hurdles to jump over, but we must learn to overcome them. Life challenges can be upsetting, even debilitating, and sometimes those challenges don't go away until you've learned the lesson they bring. That may even involve a similar situation repeating itself until you get the message, but once you understand that learning is a normal part of life, you can break free from that prison of limits. Once you realise you deserve to be happy a world of possibilities opens.

Admittedly, I have put myself in situations that dampened my spirit and were not good for me. Why? I just seemed to slip into them without taking the time to think about what I was doing. After separating from my children's dad, for example, quickly followed a disastrous relationship. It wasn't for me, but I stayed there for a while, until I soon realised that it was going nowhere and chose to end it. At that point it felt like getting into another relationship was not for me either, so I decided to enjoy a life of singledom for a few years instead. I decided to focus solely on raring my young children and started a little dance fitness business, while also taking the time for some "personal growth". The children's dad, who had always been very present in their lives, moved away and settled in with a new partner. Time passed, the children grew to be teenagers (another challenging time) and with that came their independence.

I began thinking maybe it was time to be open to idea of meeting someone again. I felt I had done a lot of personal growth over those years and that I had processed all the negative experiences in my life, including childhood trauma experienced growing up in the US before we moved back home to Ireland, previous relationships as a teenager, involving abuse in one and marrying another for convenient reasons, along with some of the causes behind my ultimate split from the children's father and the betrayal of my last pairing. I thought I had come to accept my life experiences and wouldn't let them affect or define me. I would just try to be a better person despite them. I felt I had become a stronger, more independent, smarter woman, doing her thing, enjoying life. How nice would it be to share that life with someone now? So, I put it out "into the universe".

Within months, an occasion came about, and another new journey began for me. I knew of him from the old neighbourhood and at this sombre event we got talking. I learned he had been separated for many years within the family home and had only announced a few months previously to family and friends they were officially separating. Ironically, that was not long after I spoke "to the universe", so, to me it seemed like synchronicity was at play, I'm kind of into that sort of thing, and sounded like their circumstances were a done deal.

Another occasion presented itself a few months later and we got talking more, exchanged numbers and kept in touch. Eventually, we arranged an official date several weeks later. All seemed above board. However, as reality set in with them about separating and moving from the family home, things seemed to become tenuous. The first of many scribbles on the wall that I ignored my gut on.

Initially this emerging relationship was exciting. I was ready for a new relationship and he was ready to be free again, but in hindsight neither of us really took on board the other's life position at that time. As our relationship progressed, I got caught up in trying to help with various challenges that came about. He had faced many before we met that were still raw, the recession, moving houses, deaths, etc. There was a lot of challenges to deal with at the time. I understood that separation can be difficult as I had been through a couple myself. I was very familiar with the stress and hardship it can cause, never mind dealing with the other stuff. However, I've come to learn, when the brain is in a high emotional state, be it euphoric, sad or indifferent, logic goes out the window. Like the saying goes, love is blind. Infatuation took over and looking back now it prevailed over reason.

Unfortunately, amongst all the chaos I forgot to care for myself. Lisa got lost.

The relationship was not like other relationships. It wasn't celebrated or announced. Instead it was agreed to keep it low key and very much in the background so others on his side could get accustomed to the reality of his separation. Naively, I thought I could be a good support for him during that difficult time, and perhaps I was to a point. I sympathised with his situation. Now I realise that it was not a very good idea (on all levels) to allow myself to be in a relationship that was so hidden. If a relationship needs to be hidden on any level, you really shouldn't be in it. Nevertheless, I went along with "hiding" it for two years. It wasn't the time span I envisaged at all, but we never actually spoke about a time frame and we when attempted to it always seemed to stir tension. After only a few months it began to be a thorn in the side. Well, in mine at least. Initially, we moved along, it was okay, and there were some fun times, but it didn't feel right and it didn't seem like it would change. His father wasn't even to know of the relationship before he passed away as it might cause upset; his father was a traditionalist and wouldn't approve. It was something that would stick with me. I couldn't understand why I had to be essentially a secret. A friend even thought I was having an affair! I did feel like a mistress. There were many occasions I felt diminished by regular incidents of exclusion within his extended family, occasions where I couldn't be included or invited to. My self-esteem was starting to nosedive. It got too much and eventually I insisted that we stopped hiding. How could I expect anyone to respect me, and our relationship, if I didn't and he didn't? I had sacrificed my dignity for long enough. I was accepting less than I deserved. I realised I was teaching him how to treat me. With that, finally the relationship was announced, and seemed accepted by all that we were a couple. That was great but it wasn't really announced by the standard definition. Even at the three-year stage of our relationship I was asked to hide a couple framed photos of us for a housewarming in his new place should certain people see them. Annoyed at first, I sympathised and reluctantly agreed to put one away. There were many similar sacrifices and there were times I felt the frustrations of his situation were taken out on me where I would end up in tears, but I tried to be understanding and supportive. He would say he felt the same, that I took my frustrations over caring for my mother and issues with my son out on him. We just seemed to clash.

There were some good moments but as time in our relationship marched on, the negatives started to outweigh the positives and the good times were dimmed. Despite some of his best efforts at times, in his way, I didn't feel he valued me or the relationship enough to make the changes that were necessary, that I needed in order to feel secure, loved and respected. Maybe he was just unable to. But still I stayed, not grasping the lesson, one I should have learned from the past. The pattern of relationship difficulties was repeating itself, but this time it got out of hand.

Like others, I enjoyed having a few drinks when an occasion arose, but slowly my drinking expanded into seven nights a week. Drinking was a regular part of the relationship and it was excessive at times. I began to dislike the regularity of it and the next morning drudge. It became custom for me to have a Solpadine at the ready to take first thing, due the ongoing headaches and body aches. I believe it contributed to some of the terrible arguments and incidents that became insulting and degrading at times, from both of us, as I started to become more vocal.

As a dance fitness instructor, I always liked to feel fit. I had been happy with my appearance before our union but even though I tried to stay as active as I could, I still managed to gain over two stone. There's no other way of saying it, I let myself go. The ongoing stress and anxiety I felt from all areas of my life were taking their toll. I was in a rut. I felt depressed. Feeling depressed was something I have dealt with on and off in my life, I suppose for obvious reasons. I was becoming very unhappy. I withdrew from friends and events, even ones that I had committed to doing. I suspect that due to consistent grievances over my relationship, some friends retreated. I think I would talk to anyone who would listen. On many occasions my daughter was privy to the immense hurt I was feeling, finding me in tears, because I couldn't hide it, and would do her best to try and console me. I leaned on her way too much while she herself was dealing with a very toxic relationship. I should have been there for her, not the other way around. The irony, when I was there for her, was that I would give solicited advice to her and yet wouldn't heed my own advice! She finally ended her relationship. I was so proud of her and, even though still painful, I admired the mature way she handled it. Yet, I carried on, almost embarrassingly. Why? I questioned and doubted myself. Did I love this person, or did it just become a battle of wills? What was keeping us together?

As the years rolled by, I grew increasingly frustrated. I wanted us to move on more quickly and I felt he was still in go-slow mode. We were unable to make any further commitments together, financial or otherwise, while waiting for the circumstances to be resolved. For me it was like we were hanging in limbo, with no real direction, just plodding along, not having boundaries for others or ourselves. Most attempts to talk about the situation resulted in tension, being shut down, somehow that I was crossing a line. I would say, 'it should be you and me versus the problem, not you versus me', or vice-versa. It was suggested that

I manipulated and bullied my way through the relationship, that I was the cause of the anxiety felt each morning, that I was the problem or had the problem with issues and circumstances. I began to think and say, *if* that were true, I shouldn't be in this relationship. No relationship should be based on someone bullying and manipulating their way through in effort to make it work. His status didn't bother him so why did it bother or let it bother me. It bothered me because I wanted to move on. For me enough time had been invested. It seemed that our initial infatuation had turned into a habit for companionship and little else. When the ongoing issues were pushed aside, albeit temporarily, and it was just him and I, it did seem like a good union, but the reality of the situation was that we didn't have a healthy relationship for several reasons.

As I became more and more self-aware, I began pulling away and I believe he may have too. I wanted to change, I wanted to stop drinking so much, lose weight, be more active, and I wanted to travel more. I talked about travelling a lot, where he felt I excluded him, but I think now looking back, I wanted to run away from everything. And now I wonder was that what I subconsciously thought would fix the problems, like years ago as a child when we up sticks and moved to Ireland, to escape the bad experiences. I didn't want to stay in a toxic relationship.

There needed to be change one way or another, together or not. I was physically and mentally exhausted, and I think he was too. I was getting to the point of not caring at all but still aggravated by what was going on. Our difficulties were constantly on my mind and interfered with many aspects of my life, like work, home, caring for my mother, being present for my own adult children. I was starting to resent the position I put myself in or maybe more to the point, not taking myself out of. Feeling stuck, I was desperate to figure my life out, find some guidance to get back to my old self again and part of me felt it was going to be difficult to do, if I stayed in that situation, because it wasn't changing quick enough for me and it wasn't working. After 5 years, we were heading for our sixth Christmas together and the curtain came down. An occasion occurred with extended family from which I felt excluded. This caused more stress and made me really question everything about the present and future. The attempt to talk about it led to heated discussions, and a disparaging remark that finally brought the straw to the camel's back, ultimately ending the relationship.

During the latter part of our time together, I sought to learn more about relationships and how they work. I learned that it's impossible to be emotionally ready or available to enter a new relationship when just leaving another. He wasn't ready when we met, of course. Maybe, neither was I really. He needed time to deal with and work through the separation, the process and all that goes with it, sadness, guilt, anger, along with the previous life events that happened.

It was like he came out of a prison into the prison yard with the gate wide open. Instead of waiting for him on the outside, or just walking past it, I got in there with him. I kept trying to persuade him towards that open gate, but he wasn't ready. So, I stayed in there with him, roaming around the yard, biding time, waiting, pushing, coaxing, fighting. Every now and then we'd step outside and felt what it would be like not to have that prison wall around us, all the issues that surrounded us, and it was good. There were some good times, notwithstanding the other issues needing to be addressed. But we'd end up back in the prison yard, me always wanting to get out more often and eventually permanently.

Hindsight is indeed wonderful. I wish I had the foresight to mind myself more in all this. It was becoming clearer to me that I hadn't respected and valued myself enough. I hadn't worked on deciding my own values and setting boundaries before getting into a new relationship. In those five years together, I became more unhappy with myself, acting out in ways that was troubling and confusing, contributing to the turmoil for us both... it wasn't me. The relationship did not start out on a healthy footing and what followed was a lot of energy going into the circumstances surrounding it, not into the relationship itself as it should be.

When I look back at my life, I moved from one place to another, one relationship to another, one trauma to another, but I never properly took stock and stopped to allow myself to breathe or grieve. I just kept going in the hope things would work out. It was suggested to me recently that break-ups are like grieving the death of a loved one. I never thought of it that way. I've not had someone close to me pass away yet, except my granny when I was thirteen, but I have gone through breakups. It's horrible, no matter what. The feelings of sadness I felt for the time that was invested in the relationship, of the hurt and anger have subsided. I'm working on forgiving and valuing myself more. Was there a lesson to be learned through all this? Perhaps this and all the other experiences were to teach me that it is okay to stop, to grieve and feel, to show me that I don't need to run away from feelings. I have learned to question how I showed up in relationships that enabled poor treatment. Why did I accept those situations I put myself in? My values needed to be clearer. Values often come from past pain and therefore can change over time. My boundaries also needed to be clearer. I needed to take responsibility for my own growth and happiness in all aspects of my life. I've come to see parallels of the relationships I've had. I unintentionally get involved with people who need "assistance", so in turn I guess I subconsciously avoid assisting myself.

Right now, I'm on the road to feeling strong and empowered again. A work in progress, as they say, but I feel great! I've returned to my desired weight; eating more healthily and drinking a lot less alcohol, resulting in a few extra bob in my pocket. I feel better having taken up yoga and meditating, being more active and exercising more, reconnecting with old friends and making new ones, and planning travels! And it works! It really does! I'm learning to look after myself, to be mindful of me – properly this time! When I come across a situation that I'm not sure how to handle, I ask myself 'what can I do, what can't I do?' I stop to breathe and evaluate.

I'm still teaching dance fitness, which seems to bring a lot of joy to those I come in contact with, I look after my mother (albeit in the nursing home), and I help out at a local *crèche,* which brings a smile and laughter to my day with the kids. I'm considering my options now regarding what field of business I would like to explore, what am I passionate about, what kind of goals I want to achieve. A New York move could even be on the cards! Life is a voyage for everyone, and I wish good will and much happiness for his too.

When we look back on life, we may see the pain, heartache and mistakes, but now when we look in the mirror, let's see our strength, learned lessons and pride in ourselves. Life is too short to be anything other than happy! Don't let past hurts stop an amazing future. Learn from them and create new ways of living that support you. It's okay not to have all the answers, it's okay to not have it all figured out. We are all learning and we will all continue to learn. Just check in with yourself often. 'Is this good for me or not?' Listen to your heart, listen to your gut and take logic with you! Live your truth and be the best you can be.

A Sprinkling of Some Favourite 'Fairy Dust'

"Imagine meeting someone who wanted to learn your past not to punish you, but to understand how you needed to be loved."

"Don't judge me on my past, I don't live there anymore."

"Respect is the cornerstone of compassion and love, without it positivity will not be nourished."

"A healthy relationship is where two independent people just make a deal that they will help the other person be the best version of themselves."

"Those who get upset when you try to set boundaries, are the ones who benefited the most from you having none."

"There is a message in the way a person treats you... just listen."

"Sometimes the most important lessons are the ones we've learned the hard way."

“It’s hard to fall in love again when you’re still attached to your past. Learn to let go.”

“Not everyone is meant to be in your future. Some people are just passing through to teach you lessons in life.”

“No relationship is ever a waste of time. If it didn’t bring you what you want, it taught you what you don’t want.”

“I didn’t quit. I simply chose myself, instead of continuing to try for someone who wouldn’t (or couldn’t) try for me.”

“New beginnings are often disguised as painful endings.”

“The best project you will ever work on is you.”

“The beauty of life is, while we cannot undo what is done, we can see it, understand it, learn from it and change so that every new moment is spent not in regret, guilt, fear or anger but in wisdom, understanding and love.”

Freedom of Choice

By Breeda Hurley

I have been in business since I was thirty years of age, I'm now sixty-nine! Before that I was a stay-at-home Mom with three children and before that I worked for someone who often remarked that I was a born businessperson on account of my dedication and work ethic. That comment wasn't lost on me and I knew one day that I would be an entrepreneur, even though I had no secondary or third level education; I grew up in 1950s Ireland where most children were lucky if they finished primary school before being sent out to work. Being the eldest of eight, my full-time working life began at fourteen years of age.

The road to my dream wasn't a straight one; it had many bends and detours that brought me from local shopkeeper to home-baker to restaurateur to cleaner. I also went on to have five more children and juggled running a business and home life. The cleaning venture was to prove to be my most successful and earned me several awards, one of which was *the Lifetime Achievement Award for Women in Business* in 2016.

I was good at cleaning because I was thorough; my motto was and still is, '*Our work is our pride*.' I did a short *Start Your Own Business* course with the Enterprise Board where I learned the various aspects of running a business, including the importance of closing sales, which is the mainstay for any company. I began the business with my husband Sean, and we had £74 in the bank, the year was 1995. We couldn't afford advertising, but I approached a local builder, Ned O' Shea, who was completing a housing estate in Dingle. I asked him if he would give us some work and assured him that he wouldn't be disappointed. From there, word of mouth began to spread, and our clientele started to grow. I also loved the thrill of 'cold-calling' and the buzz of selling our service since I was confident that what we were offering stood out from the rest. Our unique selling point was that I would guarantee the highest standard of cleaning and we always kept our word. We turned up on time, on the specified dates and every job was inspected by a supervisor afterwards. We listened to our clients and what they asked for; our work was of a consistently high standard. Above all, we always ensured that the customer was happy. The company which we named ABC Cleaning grew from strength to strength. As with many businesses it fluctuated with the economy but in prosperous times, we employed 364 people across most counties in Ireland and we had offices throughout Munster. Even through the choppy waters of the recession ABC Cleaning held its head above water and is today still a viable and successful business twenty-five years on.

Life was hectic with plenty of challenges, the personal kind that face us all at some point and plenty originating from my business choices. In 2017 I catalogued my journey in a memoir, called *Survive and Thrive, the Journey of a Lifetime*. Until then, I didn't appreciate how many times I'd been knocked back but each time I got up, dusted myself off and kept moving forward towards my goal, which was to be the Ultimate Entrepreneur! And on the night of my book launch I felt that I had finally reached the top step of the ladder. Author and columnist Billy Keane described the book as *"Angela's Ashes meets Roddy Doyle and it's as good a book that I have read in a long, long time."* Best-selling author and life coach, Donna Kennedy, said *"Breeda's book will change lives."*

My message is, no matter what your background, what kind of upbringing you've had or what personal challenges you've faced, you can achieve what you want in life. My key ingredients have been resilience, self-belief, determination and hard work and my greatest teachers have been my *mistakes.* Learn from them and move on.

These days I devote much of my time to inspiring people to be the best they can be in both business and life. I have overcome my fear of public speaking and now I travel the country addressing groups about what it takes to succeed. I don't read from a textbook, what I have to say comes from my heart; it is the raw truth of my journey. This chapter is entitled Freedom of Choice because I believe we all have choices and the freedom to make them. The choices we make create the twists and turns in our life's journey, but I have learnt that the best choices are made from a few simple ingredients that help us to make informed and intelligent decisions and I want to share these with you.

Self-Love

If I was given a euro for every time I heard the phrase, "she's in love with herself" or "he's full of himself" I'd probably never have had to work a day in my life. These were the dreaded phrases that I never wanted said about me. Being in love with oneself conjures up images of an unbearable personality that smothers all others in the same room. Self-love is different to that, self-love is caring about the needs of *self* and realising that when the *self* has been tended to, I can now tend to those around me with genuine love. For this reason, I believe an opposing facet of self-love is 'people-pleasing.' I used to be a people-pleaser with a '*never say no*' ethos. People-pleasing has a lot to do with worrying about what other people think of us. It is our innate need to be liked, to fit in, but it can also be very damaging resulting in a loss of *self*. I had actually forgotten that I had a name, other than *Mom*. This may be hard to believe but the first time someone outside of my family offered to make me a cup of tea I had to excuse myself from the room as my reaction was, *I don't deserve this.* I was attending a meeting and I didn't feel worthy of the attention. I realised then how low my self-esteem was. What had brought me to this place? I had thrown myself into family and working life and completely forgotten who Breeda Hurley really was. Getting to re-know Breeda wasn't an easy journey, we fell in and out of love on a number of occasions. Sometimes it does take an external event for us to fully comprehend our own value. For me, this happened when I won the Lifetime Achievement Award. That night my husband Sean gave a speech and said the most profound words I had heard in relation to me: 'Breeda has a problem saying no, she puts everybody before herself.' Those words resonated deeply with me. They didn't make me feel proud of who I was – they made me question the value I had placed on myself and I knew then that I'd had enough! I was done proving myself to everyone else, trying to earn favour by always being obliging, attending events I didn't want to go to, picking up errands for people when I had a hundred other things to do myself, the list goes on...

From that night on I never looked back and I realised that *I* mattered. That same month, I was fortunate to bump into an inspiring man called Pat Falvey. We were both invited to speak at the Women's Empowerment Summit in Dublin. It was my first time speaking to a large group and I was riddled with nerves before I got on the podium but found my voice within a few moments of starting to speak. Pat and I found common ground when we realised we were both from County Kerry. Pat is a man of many talents; he is an adventurer, an author, an inspirational speaker and highly regarded mentor and coach at a global level. In the months that followed Pat took me under his wing. He gave me the tools to convince myself that I was brilliant! Each morning I would stand before my own mirror, raise my fist triumphantly and say aloud many times "You are a wonderful woman." In the early days I would cringe at my reflection and feel stupid at the sound my voice saying these alien words. However, as time went by, I became more comfortable with Breeda in the mirror and the repetition eventually made the words sink in.

I began to notice changes in my behaviour. For example, when a friend rang me and asked for a lift into town, I said no, that it didn't suit me at that time. Our phone call ended a little abruptly for she wasn't used to me ever refusing her a *favour*. I did feel guilty and worried that she'd think less of me. However, once I got through the initial discomfort, the feelings of guilt for putting my own needs first began to subside and I noticed that people started treating me with more respect. I also noticed that loved ones developed an 'independence' and no longer relied on me to do so much and I wondered if my 'people-pleasing' had also been a way of disabling others, of making them dependent on me as a form of self-validation that I am needed, I'm of use and I'm of worth to others. So, here is my point, self-love is not selfish, but people-pleasing can be; because we do it out of fear, to be liked and to be loved but in actual fact there are no winners. Until we can love ourselves only then can we truly love those around us, and we can all experience fulfilled lives.

Trust

One day when I was five years old, an ambulance with a nurse arrived outside my home. It was September and I had just started school three weeks earlier. I don't remember the small details of that day, but the nurse showed an uncanny interest in me. I was unaware of what was happening but intrigued about the doll that the nurse was promising me in return for my accompanying her somewhere. My mother took my hand and led me outside to the ambulance. I was taken to a children's hospital in Foynes in Co. Limerick that specialised in treating children with tuberculosis. I hadn't been aware I was sick, apart from a cough that wouldn't go away. The previous May my mother's last remaining brother had died of the same disease and he had convalesced in our home for the last three weeks of his life. Little did I know that our home had become an incubator for the disease! I spent fifteen months in that hospital. One day I discovered that my brother had also been brought to the hospital, though we had little interaction as the disease was still too severe in my brother. During that time, we had no visitors. Every day I thought about the doll and each night as my head hit the pillow, I prayed that tomorrow the doll would come to me. It was as if the doll would provide the comfort and love that I was missing from my mother, the banter with my siblings; she came to represent home and everything I had been familiar with. I never got my doll. Though she never manifested, she was to have a lasting effect on me – my ability to trust had been shattered. In later years, I found it very difficult to trust anyone but myself. In addition to this, I never wanted to let anyone down. While this may sound like a highly positive trait, it actually turned me into a micro-manager or more bluntly, a 'control-freak.' I was convinced that no one could do anything as good as me. This made the early days of my business very difficult, as I tried to spread myself across all aspects, from salesperson to cleaner to accountant to human resources and so on. By the third year of the business it was clear that there was vast opportunity for growth, but my trust issues had become the pot that kept the plant root-bound. Our work force had to grow, or we were going nowhere. I found it hard to delegate at first, but I soon learned that other people flourished when I learned to give them my trust. Gradually, I became comfortable with spreading my trust and as I did so, the company flourished too, and I gained a new sense of freedom.

Trust is a vital component of love, you put it out there and hope it's cherished and never abused. Most of us consider ourselves trustworthy and reliable but giving our trust to someone else can be the challenging part. Without that ability to trust others, our lives become severely restricted and our choices are limited. Most of us have had our trust broken at some stage of our lives. It's important to acknowledge it when it happens so that we can learn but we also have to move on.

When you release your fears, and put your trust in others, you also trust in the greater good of the universe. Without this it is impossible to take risks, to undertake new ventures and to reap the many rewards. Like a healthy investment fund, trust put out into the universe returns dividends. I have a saying, that you must throw a sprat to catch a salmon. In 1999 I procured a local cleaning contract with a large national company. Our price was so low (the sprat), that the manager called me in for an interview. I promised him I could do the job and I told him I was looking at the bigger picture (the Salmon). After the first six months we secured the cleaning contract for all of Munster for the next five years.

Sometimes trust is all we have, and our gut can be our greatest trust barometer. For this reason, it's vital that we are in tune with and develop our gut instinct. Self-love, which I discussed earlier, is a first vital step in this process. Nowadays, scientists have proven a connection between our gut and our brain that is controlled by the bacteria that live in our gut. Maybe someday scientists will find gut instinct and we'll be able to take supplements to improve it! But in the meantime, the more aware we are of who we are and the more we practice self-love, we increase our intuition/gut instinct and our ability to trust in ourselves, in others and in the universe.

Twenty-three years after my experience in the hospital in Foynes, I finally got my doll. As I left the maternity hospital in 1977 with my precious first daughter, I asked my husband Sean to take me to Caballs toy shop in town. There I bought the most beautiful doll. She was for my daughter, but she was also for me.

Gratitude

We hear about the importance of gratitude every day with the belief that being grateful for the small stuff will eventually lead to the big stuff. But there're more to gratitude than that. When we fail to immerse ourselves in gratitude, we actually enter victim territory. Think of the person, who hates their job, hates their boss, hates their work colleagues, and feels hard-done by at every turn. Have you ever noticed that these people continuously attract negative circumstances? They believe they are the victims of these circumstances, but in truth they are victims of their own mindset, what I call an unhealthy mindset. Some people genuinely find themselves in terrible situations but I'm not talking about these genuine cases.

I believe the first level to gratitude is acceptance, accepting our circumstances no matter what they are. From there we have freedom to make choices. The next level to gratitude is feeling genuine gratefulness for the good in our lives. It can be hard to switch on gratitude at will, it doesn't always come easy. If things aren't going well, it's very difficult to feel grateful. But gratitude requires constant nourishment, which is being grateful for the small things. I feel grateful for having the time for a long bath, candles lighting and a glass of wine. I love meeting friends for coffee. I love watching the robins outside my window amongst the greenery of my garden, along with a host of other little treasures. These are examples of the small things that I am grateful for every day. These keep my mind healthy. In the past, I was slow to give myself permission to indulge in such things because I felt every moment had to be given over to the business and I was simply too busy to notice the simple, yet beautiful things happening around me. I am so grateful to have my husband Sean by my side, for supporting me through good and bad, and for my children and grandchildren who bring such variety to my days. Gratitude keeps your mental health clean so that when life doesn't go your way, you have fuelled your mind with the nourishment it needs to tackle any obstacle. Then you can turn a negative into a positive; this could simply mean seeing the good as well as the bad or in other words, spotting the opportunities! In terms of business, there were times when we didn't acquire certain contracts. Initially, this would seem like a major blow, not only from the financial perspective but also from the point of view of not attaining high profile clients. However, we would soon realise that such contracts were nonviable and would have compromised the future of the business. Not attaining these contracts actually gave us the scope to re-address our business model and increase our potential client-base, in other words, a negative becomes a positive.

Practice gratitude every day and surround yourself with like-minded people because it's very easy to fall into negative thought patterns. Be ruthless in the company you keep – for it becomes your reflection before you realise it – cut negative people loose. I have a little ritual that I practice when needed: if I find myself in negative company, I tap my shoulder to remind myself not to let their words and demeanours influence me. And remember, *GRATITUDE* is the *reaction* to life that keeps the *victim at bay so the victor can play*!

Self-acceptance

Self-acceptance is something that evolves as we mature, it is essential to a fulfilled life but can be hard to attain. A huge obstacle to self-acceptance is the desire for perfection. Because there is no such thing as perfection in the real sense of the word. The dictionary definition of the word *'perfect'* goes as follows "having all the parts and qualities that are needed or wanted and no flaws or weaknesses." Life is not designed that way because it was never meant to be. No human being has "all the parts" with "no flaws or weaknesses." In fact, no species in nature has been designed is such a way. But today's society has created a yearning for the perfect figure, family, home, career, and so on, even the perfect age! We are bombarded with images of people's perfect worlds on social media and in glossy magazines. Self-acceptance for me was a long time evolving but now that it's here and fully formed, I can finally say, I'm living the *PERFECT* life! And here I mean *perfect* in the sense of being fulfilled, I love what I do, and I only do what I love. I no longer worry about what other people think of me. This has given me the freedom to take on new projects, new experiences and to explore my full potential. At sixty-nine years of age, I'm living proof that it is never too late to start a business or embark on an adventure. Age is not an excuse to hold you back.

Another aspect of self-acceptance is knowing your limitations. This became apparent to me many years ago. My husband is a recovering alcoholic. There was a time when his drinking was very difficult. I felt that I had to shoulder a lot of the responsibility of running the business and raising the family and resentment and bitterness began to set in. I didn't understand that alcoholism is a disease. One afternoon I met a close friend and began my usual rant about poor me and all my troubles. She listened carefully. I was taken aback when she said, "Maybe it's yourself that needs help." I retorted that I had no problem and it was my husband that was the issue. She suggested I attend Al Anon for six meetings. Al Anon is a self-help twelve-step programme for spouses and families affected by alcoholism. Despite my initial protests, I found myself in a roomful of strangers one Wednesday night hoping to find the solution to stop my husband drinking. I was shaking and my cheeks were red with embarrassment. I didn't open my mouth for the whole evening, but I listened carefully for the first time in my life! I decided to attend the remaining five meetings. There I learned that my husband's drinking was none of my business and to focus on myself instead. This was a shock to learn, firstly, how could my husband's drinking not be my problem too? And secondly, I surely didn't have a problem that needed focus. But as the weeks went by, I began to learn the twelve-step programme of Al Anon. I was told that I had no control over anyone but myself. Initially, this seemed like a major limitation, how was I going to make my husband better if I had no control over him? Soon I began to feel immense relief and the bitterness and resentment started to dissipate. The group recommended I read the book *Courage to Change: One Day at a Time in Al-Anon*. This offered me a whole new way of looking at life. The children even noticed a change in my behaviour. I was amazed when they commented that Mom doesn't shout any more or give out to us. I gave up begging my husband to stay home from the pub. One day he asked why I wasn't complaining about his drinking. I said in a very calm voice that it was *none of my business*. He was taken aback. I was so proud of myself to be able to converse with him without being angry. Shortly afterwards Sean became sober.

Going to Al Anon has been one of the best decisions of my life and I still practice the twelve steps to this day. It has benefited every aspect, both personal and business. Perhaps one of the biggest lessons I learned was that accepting my limitations is a form of self-acceptance. These days, in my mentoring sessions, I tell my clients that limitations are opportunities in disguise; they push us to venture out into the world for help and in doing so we meet amazing people and broaden our horizons. Limitations are our portals to knowledge that we would otherwise fail to seek out.

Fun and the Importance of Laughter

In April 2019 I had bought cooking apples with the intention of making an apple tart. One week later the apples were still in the fridge. Sean commented, 'Are you going to do anything with them?' with an undertone of '*more waste again!*' which sparked a determination in me to get the apple tart made. At about the same time, my sister Miriam arrived as I went about preparing the ingredients. Miriam is my younger sister, she's one of the most positive people I know and is the best fun to be with. Like most of us in society these days, Miriam always has her phone in her hand. 'Will we go live? she said, with the phone already pointing at my face.

'No way,' I said, 'put that thing away.'

But not wanting to be a killjoy I said, 'Okay so, go ahead.'

Miriam immediately took on the role of TV presenter asking all the right questions about the baking process. Except that I didn't have all the right answers because I'm so used to making these tarts, I no longer have to know the correct measurements. The comments started flowing in, *Hello ladies, can you give the recipe? How much flour was that? Was that self-raising flour? How much butter?*

I couldn't believe that people were actually watching us, let alone showing interest. The apple tart went into the oven and we turned off the camera. But people wanted to see the baked apple tart so thirty minutes later we went live again!

It soon became apparent that there was an appetite for more home cooking videos from my kitchen. We set up our own Facebook page, called *Johnny's Cottage*, named after my uncle who originally owned the cottage that I now live in. We ran a live video every fortnight and we invited our sister Aine to join us as we were having so much fun. It became so popular that people wanted to see the *'show'* once a week. So, every Monday night at 7.30 pm we go live. Sometimes we all cook a dish, sometimes we take turns. I am the serious one who wants to make the "perfect" dish, but my sisters are quick to remind me that there's no such thing as perfection! Aine's honesty is tear-inducing, she is not afraid to tell the truth, if a dish doesn't turn out as planned. Miriam's dishes often end up in the bin, but she doesn't care because her dishes will never reach her own home, for none are intended for her partner, Steady Eddie!

We have never laughed so much, and I know our *show* has become staple viewing for many people who tune in to have a laugh with us. People now stop us on the street and ask what we're cooking next week or just want to thank us for cheering them up on a Monday evening, saying it's a great start to the week. So, don't be afraid of taking on new ventures for you'll never know where they might lead you or how they might enrich your life. In my wildest dreams, I never expected to be doing anything like this, but it has become an important part of my life and it has strengthened the bond between us three sisters. Without self-love and self-acceptance, I doubt I would have had the courage to let Miriam video me that first night.

Johnny's Cottage has also transformed other parts of my life. While this may sound cliché, it has taught me not to take myself so seriously and that sometimes the best thing you can do for anyone is make them smile. Now when I give one of my talks around the country, I make sure that everyone in the room is smiling or laughing before I even reach the podium. This is achieved by a dramatic entrance: me dancing up the aisle to the sound of 'Fight Song" by Rachel Platten. Many people who attend my talks may be at a crossroads in their lives, they want to try something new, improve what they have, be it business or personal. They come to learn how to switch on their courage gene or see situations in a new light. I have seen a room full of uptight shoulders relax, nervous tension lifting like a fog. There can be some bemused faces but by the time I say my first word, there is a smile across everyone's face. Laughter puts us all on the same level as each other; it breaks barriers and builds trust.

So to conclude, whether you believe we have been put here for a reason or that life is a random event, we all deserve to reach our full potential, which is ultimately to love and be loved, for surely that is the ultimate definition of success. The choices we make will determine how and when we reach it. After nearly seven decades on this earth, I believe that *Self-love, Trust, Gratitude, Self-Acceptance* and *Fun* are essential ingredients. I haven't always been aware of this for if I had I'm sure I would have avoided much hardship along my route! But then again, it is mostly the hardships which have brought me to these conclusions.

And remember; never treat your days as a rehearsal, for no day comes around a second time. Keep focused on the road ahead, not the road you've travelled. Be kind to yourself, do your best and *learn by heart* that perfection doesn't exist. Never give up on your dreams!

Don't Give Up!

by Robyn Walters

"It is not whether you get knocked down

It's whether you get back up."

– Vince Lombardi

Have you ever doubted yourself or your capability to achieve your goals? If you have, you're not alone. Most of us have, even the most "successful" of us. Most people experience hardships and knockbacks at some point in their life and it's easy to feel overwhelmed by them but for the purposes of you becoming truly empowered, I invite you to be open to the idea that it's not the hardships and knockbacks that are the problem, it's how we react to those hardships and knockbacks that makes the difference. I am proof that with the right perspectives and attitude achieving a goal is possible, no matter what your circumstances.

Today I am the proud owner of RWR Recruitment, a business that oozes honesty and integrity with a fantastic team at the forefront sharing a common goal to succeed. In year one despite the market being difficult, our team grew, we moved into a larger premises, and made a decent end of year profit. We won large recruitment tenders, signed exciting contracts with companies looking to grow on a permanent basis across the UK and implemented a recruitment formula to our industry that understood how rich the combination of skill and culture was for companies to gain a return on their investment. It is a huge success and I am very proud of its achievements to date. Using our initiative to make things happen, make decisions, and influence and persuade others, is the reason I love my profession but initiative alone was not the driving force behind my success; the determination, resilience and courage to never give up on what mattered to me was always the key to achieving. The characteristics that shaped me personally and financially to achieve my dream today can be followed back to the early stages of my life. Let me share with you the importance of not giving up on your dreams.

Even though my business is a great success to date, it wasn't always that way, it wasn't always plain sailing like it may appear, if you met me now. It truly resonates with me that being an entrepreneur is not all about waiting for the storm to pass but rather learning to bounce back, which I experienced many times throughout my life. These setbacks would have forced many to throw in the towel, yet I saw them as a series of opportunities to another yes! Without these rejections and failures in my life I wouldn't have the drive I do today!

Looking back, school was a challenging time for me. I would be foolish not to acknowledge that it had an impact. I received a bit of teasing in primary school, but in high school it was more emotional and psychological bullying, which at one point led me to not want to even go to school. I really struggled to belong to a friendship group; I found myself moving from one friendship group to another but was never really accepted. In each group I would be left out, isolated and intimidated and I received an array of nasty comments. I would just put up with the whispering behind my back, the exclusions and in-jokes and humiliation, which led me to feel unwanted, alone and hard to form trust in others, when all I wanted was to belong. Being picked on for some reason, left a lingering feeling of failure. Of course, it's not my fault but somehow, I felt it was or that at least I should have fought back at times, it knocked my confidence and in many ways was a trigger to lack of trust I developed in people. In the back of my mind I knew what was needed, I just needed to pluck up the courage. I needed a smart and self-kind way to handle the situations I was facing and instead of letting them lead me to self-doubt and dragging me down into negativity for days or even weeks, I simply kept going. Fortunately, at home I was surrounded by constant love, compassion and encouragement from my family which motivated me to keep trying in school, and in sixth form I found a soul mate whom I am still friends with today that really changed my school experience to a more positive journey.

Reflecting on life now, I am very lucky that the support and encouragement from my family and boyfriend has always been very strong. Even though knockbacks in life can be challenging, I always had my family around for emotional support. In particular, I see my mother, father and sister as true inspirations and have always been grateful for their opinions and support to guide me in the right direction. Even if at times they questioned me, when I decided to start RWR my dad asked me if this was the right decision, or if going into employment would be easier for me and less of a stress, but I knew this was my passion and deep down I knew I wasn't going to give up – I wanted to prove to myself I could succeed in this career. With that said, my family stuck by my decision and without their support I would not reach for the remarkable. I was blessed, as often I would be stressed and exhausted when we all met up as a family, as conversations for me were often weighed down by my own self-doubt as to how payroll would be met the following month, and when I would hit the glorious target of cashflow I envisaged but my family understood. You must never take for granted their deep commitment to you, as their help will never show on your income statement, but they are a true asset of my business journey that I will be forever grateful for.

The lack of trust I kept feeling was reinforced through my adult life such as difficulty forming and maintaining relationships as I just wanted the perfect relationship, yet no matter how loyal I was, it sadly wasn't reciprocated. The next hurdle I faced was university. In 2009 I embraced the university lifestyle moving up north to Manchester, which was about a four-hour-drive from home. A fresh start, meeting new people with the expectation that I would have the best time of my life. Everyone tells you that you'll form loads of friendships in fresher's week but very quickly, my first year in university became a big disappointment. I was optimistic about making friends and living in this big city, but like in my past I began feeling lonely within the first few weeks of moving into my student accommodation, I felt pressure to stick with the people I lived with in my halls, even though I had no connection with them, and the long distance relationship I had really influenced me to choose travelling home a lot over the weekends. At the end of first year, people started to discuss in their halls and fresher groups who they would move in with in second year. This was a conversation I feared and felt anxious about, knowing I didn't really click with anyone in my halls. I remember speaking with the university lecturer, requesting if it was possible for me to move to a university closer to home as this feeling was all too familiar. It is easy to feel embarrassed when you feel this way, especially in an era where social media is a huge part of our lives, watching everyone posting their amazing experiences online at university, it can be hard to admit your loneliness when others are managing to make friends and go out with ease. But then I saw an advert in a shop window where a group of girls were looking for a housemate, I knew this was my opportunity.

Shortly after moving into my new digs, I was starting to enjoy university a little more as the girls I was living with were really friendly. It was just a huge shame that they were all from Manchester, as on weekends they would travel back to their friends and family and I would be alone, at a time when I would have appreciated socialising with them the most. So, once again I found myself feeling quite lonely when the weekends came along. After a university lecture one day, I saw a huge queue outside Manchester Hall. Being nosy, I went over to have a little look at all the commotion. Little did I know that day I would be joining in and signing myself up to participate in a summer placement at Camp America. In this hall, were hundreds of different USA camp representatives, each telling you all about what their camp had to offer and why you should volunteer to attend their camp. It was mind blowing! I filled out lots of different applications that day as it really intrigued me, although deep down thinking that nothing would come of it. A few months later, I received a letter from *Racquets Lake Camp* in New York advising that I had been selected to teach tennis at their private girl's summer camp for summer 2011. I was shocked, I assumed I had not been selected, yet excited about the prospect of heading to USA at the age of twenty to teach a sport I was passionate about from such a young age. I absolutely loved tennis and thanks to my mum, I had the opportunity to play tennis across the UK at a competitive level after school and over weekends since the age of 16. I think the sport not only gave me credibility where local players wanted to play against me, it also gave me a huge boost in confidence, knowing I would go out on the court, time and time again winning, would leave me feeling I could achieve anything. This feeling was polar opposite to when I was in school and no matter how good I felt on the court, in school I didn't have that sense of credibility from my peers that I longed for. I found the sport a great release for me, I was always focused when playing but most of all had fun on the court and appreciated the joy of hitting, moving and competing, which my parents and coaches assisted me with. I adopted qualities when playing the sport, such as focus, fun and being mentally tough, qualities that are truly ingrained within me and assisted me in my business growth outside of sport. I strongly believe that the older I got I accepted that I deserved every win I had, not knowing back then that the level of competitiveness I had and still have to this day has had a massive impact and huge advantage in my business career.

Camp America was an incredible experience; putting on a backpack at age twenty and heading to the unknown was daunting but the experience pushed me out my comfort zone and gave me a huge amount of responsibility. I became a leader, a role model, without even noticing it! The USA visa enabled me to have a few months to travel around America if we wished, once the placement finished. I was very fortunate to be offered to stay with a family I met on Parents' Day at Camp in New York to begin my adventure and plan my journey. Solo travelling was a scary thought at first, arriving not knowing anyone and at times I was scared of the unknown. Moving from big buzzing cities to stunning national parks, numerous internal flights alone, chilled out beaches to classic American towns but I became independent and left with a whole group of new friends that I had met along my travels. The experience taught me to be resilient, adaptable and driven, to embrace change and new environments. My summer adventure came to an end and I was heading back to University in September to complete my final years and this was when university life really began for me. I bet you're thinking, what was different? Well, I met a girl on my course who asked me to go shopping with her after a lecture. With no hesitation, I took her up on this! I didn't realise that day, that such a small gesture would shape my future time at university, and it really reminded me that I am not a quitter! I am grateful for the friendship I formed that day and excited to say this time next year I will be sharing her very special day as her bridesmaid.

After graduating with a 2:1 at the University of Manchester I set out on a travelling adventure, my backpack and I, an adventure of a lifetime that saw incredible cultures, people and ways of life. Although twelve months after embarking on my big breakout journey across the southern hemisphere, I found myself back at home licking my wounds with no concrete career path in comparison to my highflying peers, the majority of whom were in high band levels of the NHS. I was stuck; I really didn't know what the future had in its hands for me. I vividly remember the day I cried to my dad, feeling uncertain of my path yet with his great words of wisdom, I realised that I needed to know what my goals were in life, what was important to me? What did I want from the career I chose? My self-exploration was simpler than I imagined. I knew my end goal was to be financially richer to provide the best life for my immediate family, so I googled what job made the most money the quickest and recruitment was in that top five. After exploring what characteristics and skills were required to be a recruiter, I felt this was the path I was destined to follow. My journey through recruitment began.

I worked for numerous national recruitment firms gaining great insight into the industry, which I thoroughly enjoyed. Being naturally bullish and impatiently ambitious I always wanted to run before I could walk to reach my end goal in my career. When the opportunity arose to start a business venture with one of my close friends it was a no-brainer. It was an exciting time, but I hadn't been in the recruitment industry that long, so it was daunting at the same time. My friend had been offered to set up a recruitment business with an established businessman and after some negotiation we were both to be shareholders and directors on the board of the new firm. My friend and I had been colleagues in a competitive recruitment environment for a firm prior to this venture, so we knew a lot about each other's professional strengths and weaknesses and how we cope with pressure. We found that our different ways of approaching things really complimented one another in business and motivated us to keep moving forwards however, as for business plans, we pretty much made it up as we went along to be honest! We had many ups and downs setting up the business, but we were so proud and excited to be recruitment directors, creating a brand, website and logo to launch into the market. A few months into the journey we had secured our high street offices, decorated, and taken on another staff member. Having an investor in our business didn't come without its challenges. Unfortunately, in the background things were not adding up, I was very clued in when it came to tracking our progress and figures and noticed that the investor was not as transparent as we once thought and we were putting a lot of time and effort into this firm and I didn't want to continue to do so, knowing that we would not reap the rewards. At the time, my friend could see my frustration and there were even instances where our investor would manipulate the truth telling me one thing and my friend another to gain control. As time passed, it became very clear that the main purpose of such lies and manipulation was to split me and my business partner up. Trying to put a wedge between us to drive us apart, which backfired as my friend and I were stronger than ever trusting each other's judgements. I knew within a short time after setting up this venture that we could make it a success in the industry, so I suggested we go to the bank and seek advice on funding to set it up completely on our own. Having a tendency not to trust people, stemming from my earlier years, I felt that our first experience proved that we needed to take this into our own hands without reliance on others.

Unfortunately, my friend was not in agreement with this idea and wanted to engage with another investor. After much deliberation, going against my own intuition, I reluctantly agreed to meet with whom would be our next business investor. We were fortunate to secure a deal with the (silent) business investor who shared half the business with us to begin with to assist us with the finances to start up. And so, our second chance at building a recruitment business together began. We moved into a warehouse within the investors premises and started over, reentering the workforce and rebranding our name. The business went from strength to strength in the first six months but unfortunately, I found myself working relentless hours on my own with little input from my friend as her attention was not focused on the business at the time. Our investor caught wind of her lack of participation and sadly it did not end well. She was forced to leave the board. Sadly, when under the pressure of losing her position I felt she threw me under the bus, which as a close friend I never thought would happen. It opened my eyes. Once again, I felt back in a position where my trust had been broken. It was a shame, but I learned in that moment that the only people who had my back was my family and me. I had devoted my time to make this business a success. I knew I was not going to give up. It was a sad moment to lose a friend, but I only wanted people in my life that were genuine, and I moved on, ploughing all my attention into work and reassuring the team that the business was okay and moving forward. This meant that the business was split between the investor and I. Going forward without my friend was daunting and a decision I really didn't want to happen, but I still had the business I worked so hard towards. I was put, yet again, in a precarious situation where my trust still had to lie in another person, the investor. At this point in time, it reiterated my gut feeling that I couldn't trust anyone. Looking back now at this situation, I think some people are destined to be either an employee or entrepreneur and there is nothing wrong with being one or the other, I just found myself being the latter.

When it came to the business there were many challenges but invaluable lessons, as the challenges I faced as a business owner with little support were tough. Many times, I doubted what I was doing, such as restructuring to adapt the business to the changing market, on-boarding the right staff, leadership, staff meetings, chasing debtors etc., an endless list. I questioned what the hell I was doing more often than not but always came back harder, stronger and more determined to make the business a success. When feeling overwhelmed I learnt to stay focused on the end game and to believe in my own abilities, to create mini plans to make the necessary changes to move forward and never give up, no matter how tough things were!

In year three business was really starting to flourish, I think I surprised myself that we would be out of the original cold, dreary warehouse we began in and in a high street office space with a huge team behind us and all initial investment paid back. I felt the team were stable and moving in the right direction, so I made the decision to go on holiday, a one week break out of business to Turkey for the first time within the three years running. I was so excited to spend some quality time with my boyfriend and best friends. It was a nerve-wracking feeling, leaving the business for a whole week but I felt it was ready for me to do so. My business partner at the time was not involved in the daily operations of the business; in fact he rarely was involved in the business at all, although I always thought it was professional to keep him in the loop and asked if he could keep an eye on the office in my absence, touching base with the team on regular occasions. Little did I know, he was waiting for such an opportunity to arise. The high-flying business I left behind would not be the same again! In my absence, the business was being tarnished with lies and manipulative comments, turning staff members against me and breaking up the great team that was established.

You could say I was naive, too trusting or perhaps it was ignorance to my business partner's years of experience in being an entrepreneur that led me to sign off some decisions that would bite me in a situation I found myself in whilst abroad. Back at the beginning of the business venture my business partner requested that his "side kick" was also on the board of directors and as I got on well with him and trusted in his professionalism, I simply agreed that this wouldn't be an issue, therefore at the time of my holiday there was three directors and two split shareholders, one being myself. Two days into my holiday in Turkey I received a call from my business partner, a call I never expected, that led my holiday to be a disaster. Sadly, I spent my whole time in the hotel lobby, confused, worried and frustrated that my business was being torn apart with lies and manipulation and there was nothing I could do a million miles away. My boyfriend and best friends were so supportive and understanding to the situation, trying to calm my heightened emotions down, helping me to find ways to overcome the problems, comforting my tears and offering suggestions and ideas to overcome the challenges blocking my motivation. But on my return, it only got worse!

Everything I had worked so hard to build I watched disintegrate before my eyes. I felt helpless. After many long discussions and tense meetings, with the directors and my family, I decided to leave without anything. It was a tough decision as I loved my job, but my health was more important. I didn't gain anything financially from the business, in fact I lost money. I had come to a point where I just wanted out, the psychological and emotional stress and pure heartache of uncertainty was too much strain and drained me. Walking away from a business that I had put everything into was my last resort, however after much deliberation, in my eyes the business was never going to assist me in achieving my goals in such a toxic situation. I realised that I needed to value my own time and expertise and hard work over those three years. It wasn't worth wasting my positive energy on a never-ending negative situation, and after seeking legal advice the best option for me was to hand in my resignation as director. I learned so much from this entire experience but the most important thing I learned was to not give up on myself, on my passion and my goals in life. Trust in yourself and trust your gut.

The heart wrenching day that I put my big girl pants on and met with my fellow directors was an odd feeling, a mixture of emotions, both deep sadness and relief. Like anyone else, I put on a brave face and stayed strong, but I must admit, deep down I was freaking out, mainly over disbelief and self-doubt, as people in the industry saw me just leave a business. They never saw the truth as to why I left or the obvious financial worry over how I was going to pay the mortgage next month. All the promises and financial agreements made between myself and my business partner that weren't adhered to meant I didn't have the money for a legal battle, it was a strain. I may not have had the finances, but I had the internal drive and love for my profession. I set out in recruitment to gain a great lifestyle for me and my family and that is what I was going to do. I wasn't going to let a bad situation make me emotionally suffer – My mind over and over kept talking to my heart advising me to move on! Get over it and continue to succeed.

Although this wasn't as easy as it may sound. My trust had been broken on numerous occasions, not only through friendships but also in business leading me to question whether being an entrepreneur was the right role for me or whether I should accept to be an employee. Did I really have it in me to start again?

Have I got the right credentials to own a business and be successful? My trust had been compromised on several occasions leading to the loss of two businesses and making me doubt my ability. For days I had sleepless nights, worrying. I felt lost, with no purpose.

This is truly the biggest hurdle I have faced in my life, but I wasn't going to settle for anything other than success. Hitting rock bottom, reminded me of the time of when I was going to move universities and quit, I remembered this was not an option. I remembered that Camp America proved that I can go outside my comfort zone and be independent. To succeed I needed to trust in myself and not rely on others. I think this is a valuable lesson in life that would empower everyone who lives by it.

With this in mind, that week I got on the phone to Business Wales to find out all the funding options that were out there for start-up businesses and began, what felt like another university dissertation – my own business plan! Time was of the essence, when you find yourself in a negative cycle, you must break through the pattern and flip the story, so I ploughed on through my checklist to reinvent my business. By the end of week one, my business plan had been accepted and the start-up business loan was granted, which gave me a huge buzz again. I have huge gratitude at this time in my life to my sister who was a huge support mechanism in the birth of RWR and her dedication and trust in me was empowering – I am eternally grateful to her. The challenges I had faced in my previous business dynamic, and the negative effects it had on my family, made me determined to succeed more than ever. I had nothing to lose but everything to gain. I would not give up, I would not quit, no matter what. And as a result of that mindset, RWR is now an award-winning success that my team and I can take pride in. I didn't let the stress beat me. I rose above it and did what it took to create a business of integrity and honesty.

As you can see from the snippet of my journey, there will be days when you're seriously stressed yet many days where you will feel on top of the world. It can be a hard and long climb to success, but the rewards will outshine the drawbacks and it will all be worth it when you reach the top! The key really is to keep going! So, I suppose you're asking yourself... HOW?

You must learn that rejection is ok. It is not the end of the world and more opportunities will arise, if you're open to receiving them. If you don't hit your target first time, try again, but never give up! I have found that taking one step at a time and goal setting whether that be monthly, weekly or even daily goals to achieve, has helped me to stay focused in such difficult times. When you set a goal, a sense of commitment kicks in and a feeling of morale and motivation appear.

Failures and knockbacks in life aren't easy. If you have experienced it like me, you know how quickly it can turn you away from your dream goals. The resulting fear can sometimes lead you to settle for less but you're not that kind of person, are you? You're a fighter, the very reason you are reading this is because you push yourself harder than anyone else. Reaching your goals isn't always about knowledge, talent or experience, sure it helps but the motivation to put all of this into practice is what drives success. Look at each challenge in your life or business as an opportunity. You will realise that some of today's biggest failures will provide the greatest foundation for your future. Success isn't a straight line, there are often bumps along the way to challenge us, but the determination, self-motivation and inner drive is the magic. I hope my story has inspired you to pursue your dream. Don't give up, you got this!

Embrace the Caterpillar, Become the Butterfly

by Rayner Davies

I was sitting in my office on a beautiful August summer's day in 2019, quietly working my way through the 3-digit numbers of emails in my inbox, when I came across two emails with the subject line "Congratulations". Both emails were congratulating me for being selected as *Wales Top 35 Under 35 Business and Professional Women of 2019*. I couldn't believe it. I was totally blown away by this amazing news. Having my name on the list amongst such determined, successful women was breathtaking!

I sat there with the biggest smile on my blushing face, allowing myself to feel proud, a proudness that I don't often allow myself to feel. It was a huge sense of accomplishment. In that moment I could have ran around my office, waving my long bendy arms over my head, back and forth, shouting out with excitement. Of course, I didn't but that was the feeling I felt deep inside. It was a feeling of, *I CAN DO THIS, I AM DOING THIS!* 2019 sure was turning out to be one of my best years yet with several award wins, including the highly prestigious IOD Institute of Directors award where I won the Welsh title and was invited to London for the UK finals.

Rewind life to the young tender age of fifteen. I was a young girl working in a fish and chip shop, studying for my GCSEs and trying to have a life. This was all fine until suddenly and unexpectedly life as I knew it changed.

I had just completed yet another day in school, another day learning, not knowing what was sticking in my brain and what was going over my head. I headed to the local public bus station toilets in Neath, my hometown, to change into my work uniform. Keeping the old rusty steel toilet door tightly closed, I proceeded to peel back the wrapper of a pregnancy kit. I didn't know how to take a pregnancy test, so I attentively followed the instructions, step by step reading them repeatedly. I nervously waited. Two minutes had passed, which felt like hours, and there they were — two pink lines, as vertical and clear as a freshly painted racetrack. I was pregnant! I was fifteen and pregnant!

I can only describe it as a million thoughts running around my mind all at once. I couldn't focus, I couldn't think logically. I felt scared, scared of what my family would say. *What was I going to do? How was I going to cope? I must tell my parents! What will the teachers think of me?* I felt ashamed. *I couldn't fully look after myself, how was I ever going to be able to look after a baby? It's a huge commitment. It's forever. This is now my life. Did it mean it was all over for me?* All the dreams I could once see in my mind felt like they were gone, that all life's opportunities had vanished in a split second.

*

'Mum, Mum wake up, I brought some food home for you.' I whispered quietly to wake up my mum. I wanted her to come downstairs to eat the perfectly battered fish I had cooked for her. 'I'm not hungry, I'm sleeping.', she muttered. 'Please Mum, I've boiled the kettle and there is a beautiful fish waiting just for you.'

Down the stairs she walked, me in front. I made sure I took the slowest smallest baby steps, reluctantly getting to the last step. I asked her to sit down and enjoy her food. Stuttering, I tried to get the words out, 'Mum, Mum ummmm, Mum, errrrrrrr, okay, I am just going to tell you. I'm pregnant.' That was it, the beautiful fish I had cooked for her was left untouched and upstairs she ran to call my sisters. She told them to come downstairs, that it was important. There we were at 12am, myself, my mum and my two sisters, Lorna and Rebecca, all discussing what was I going to do. The biggest question was, was I going to keep my baby? We spoke for hours, crying and planning out a future that didn't look so bright and positive for me. I barely slept that night. In fact, none of us did.

The following morning, the sun beamed through the living room windows. I asked Dad if he was able to give me a lift to school. 'School?' he said, 'The F****** clinic I will be taking you!' I ran out the front door to the bus station and thought, *'That's it, my life is over, he is going to kill me.'* Thankfully, my dad didn't kill me, and months soon passed.

I'll never forget the day I walked down the long road that led to the main entrance of my comprehensive school to collect my GCSE results. There were stares from students, looking down on me, whispering and pointing at my baby bump. One teacher said, 'Well, we all know what was on your mind.' I instantly felt like a failure and I hadn't even opened the envelope that hid my grades inside. I wanted the ground to swallow me, and it didn't get much better when I opened the envelope to find I had failed my GCSEs, all bar one, for which I got a C. There I was, a pregnant teenager with not one possession to my name, and an education that wasn't going to get me very far in life. *Great!*

On a cold December evening in 2001 at 18.36 my beautiful son, Cameron, was born. The love that filled my heart, that filled my whole body, was a love only a parent can explain. It was an instant eternal love, a love I had never felt before. For any mum reading this, you know that the instant love you have for your baby is a love that burns so fierce, a love you will hold inside forever. Within the first twenty-four hours of having my beautiful baby boy I had learnt so much about myself, and the strength that I had deep down. I had barely any money; most things I bought were second-hand. I trawled through second-hand ads in the papers and this was how I started to build my life.

As much a failure as I felt to my parents, the love they had instantly for my son was a love that no matter how angry they were with me, the love took all their anger and disappointment away and turned it into happiness. At that time, I lived at home with my parents. My son's cot was cramped in my bedroom, but the bigger he got, the more things he needed. The family home just wasn't big enough for us. We needed our own space.

At ten months old my son and I started our lives independently. We moved into a tiny two bedroom cramped rented house, which had no central heating. There were just gas fires hanging on the walls. Each winter's night I would have to light the gas heaters, turning them on and off repeatedly; to get a steady heat was impossible. I was inundated with second-hand towels and curtains (they must have been from the 70's), plates, pots, pans and lots of other household necessities. But no matter how old they were or how worn they looked, I will be forever grateful for everything I had and for the generosity of family members that helped me get started.

After months of living in my home the damp smell became ever more potent, but this was my home. It was a million miles from perfect, but it was my home. The only choice I had was to make the best out of a very difficult situation. It sure wasn't what I had seen on fairy tale movies or how life was described in the fairy tale books I had read, but it was my home.

The very small group of school friends I had went to college, had nights out and did normal teen things, whilst I was at home changing diapers, winding my colic baby and having sleepless nights. To this day I remember the hurt I felt when only one of them came to see me and my baby. I was deeply upset and so disappointed. It made me feel more alone than I had ever felt before. I decided that they were not true friends. I didn't need them. No matter how lonely it got, I had my baby and he was what kept me going day in, day out.

Having no other option at the time, I embarrassedly claimed benefits, to help pay my rent, bills, council tax and food. Carefully, I calculated my weekly bills, week after week, month after month. I was counting the pennies. On the very rare occasion there was a little left over to pay for a few hours out in a play centre, but I was constantly borrowing ten pounds here and ten pounds there, ensuring every penny was paid back, until my next borrowing.

I was learning to become independent. I was learning what it was like to stand on my own two feet and at a very young age I had life skills that some people don't get until they are in their 30's at least.

As Cameron turned two, it was time to start building something better for us. His dad worked during the day, so I looked for a course that allowed me to study in the evenings. I decided I was going to become a college student in the hope it might create a better future. I was immensely inspired by the midwives that supported me through my pregnancy and delivered my baby. One midwife, Chris Doran, was simply outstanding. She filled me with so much positivity and had every faith that I was going to be an amazing mum. I wanted to become a midwife, I wanted to be just like her.

However, three months into my *Access to Health* course with one assignment already issued, I wasn't feeling well. I was vomiting and didn't seem to be able to control it. I thought it might be a sickness bug, but then I wondered — *Am I pregnant? Again? No this isn't possible! This cannot be happening.* But it sure was happening. I was having my second baby!

*

As my baby bump grew, my dreams once again disappeared. I made the decision that studying wasn't going to be possible at that time in my life. It felt like all the dreams I had at that young age were suddenly taken from me again and placed in a highly secured glass box. I could see all my dreams very much alive inside the box, swirling around, but they were impossible to touch. Those dreams were mine, but I was so far away from them being a reality.

On July 2004 at 5.03am my gorgeous little girl was born. She was so dainty, and her cry, even though it was a cry, was a beautiful cry, her bottom lip would quiver. She was just perfect. A few months passed and my money situation was tighter now than it had ever been. I was constantly juggling what bills to pay one week and what bills I could leave until the very last letter hit my hallway floor, reading in big bold red letters "Final Warning for Payment." Those final warnings took priority and another bill would not have been paid. It was constant juggling bill after bill. If you have been in this position yourself in life, you know only too well that it really isn't a nice position to be in.

At that point I decided that I had enough, I got myself into this situation and only I could get myself out of it. I needed to find a job. I needed to be earning my own money. I needed my first proper job so I could support my little family. And so, I became a care worker, supporting the elderly and disabled. Caring, loving and nurturing my two babies meant I had the perfect skills to apply to my job. I was determined. I was a mum and I had my first proper job. I was starting to build a future for me and my babies.

The hours of community care work were very long. I had to leave my home at 6.30am and on some days I didn't get back home until 11pm. There were gaps throughout my rota, which allowed me to pop back and forth to my home and see my children but not for very long. If you are a mum reading this, you may very well have experienced the challenges of childcare, working and being a mum. It's a constant juggle. I was so fortunate to have had so much help from my parents and family members who looked after my children on days I was scheduled to work. It was hard work, but it was a start, a start that got me closer to making my dreams at reality.

My dreams were huge, and I would wake up with a feeling of excitement for a split second. I dreamt of a nice house with a driveway and a garage, a nice car, the kids and I wearing nice clothes, and going to the most exotic holiday destinations. My dreams were magical. I remember it as though it was yesterday, saying to myself that before my children were teenagers, I would take them to Florida to see Mickey Mouse. This dream required thousands of pounds and at that time I didn't have a thousand pennies to spare, let alone thousands of pounds. I didn't know how I was going to pay for it, and I didn't know how it was going to happen, but sitting in my damp tiny two bedroom rented house, I made a promise to myself that this dream would come true. Living a great life was stamped in my mind as though it was already happening, I could feel the excitement in my tummy. I could see the huge smiles beaming across my children's faces. I needed to find a way to create the life I had dreamt of a reality.

However, a change of house in 2006 and a nasty break up with the children's dad meant I was a single working mum to a five-year-old and a two-and-a-half-year-old, having to juggle even more of life's challenges. I was twenty-one, not one of my dreams had come true and I was single. *Could things really get any worse?*

My children were such good little ones, every evening they would go to bed at 7pm, and from 7pm onwards I would sit downstairs allowing my thoughts to consume my mind. Most of my thoughts were negative, it was as though my mind was in a boxing ring taking punch after punch. I spiralled very quickly into what I can only describe as a deep black hole. I had been diagnosed with depression at nineteen and it felt like it was taking control of my mind once again. Following the evening routine of bathing, supper and teeth brushing, Cameron, Demi and I would cuddle in on the sofa, one tucked under my left arm and one tucked under my right arm, I would read them their favourite fairy tales, then off upstairs we would go. I would tuck them into bed, teddies, fleecy blanket, and kisses, even Eskimo kisses. Closing their doors, saying 'Night, night' (several times) and as soon as there was silence, my thoughts would immediately take control of my mind. It was like I was living my life as two completely different people.

I would sit, lonely and depressed, feeling that I wasn't good enough, that I wasn't worthy of happiness, that I was a failure, and so many other negative thoughts shouting in my mind. The thoughts were so powerful and strong, it was as though they were true, one hundred percent facts. When your mind is consumed with so much doubt and negativity it really is hard to see past the thoughts and see all the positives within your life. With tears flowing down my face I would take the sharpest of knives and cut my arms and the tops of my legs, putting slices into my skin, as though I was carving meat. The tears would flow, not from the pain of cutting, but from the stabbing emotional pain I felt inside. My mind had been taken over by the thoughts inside my head, I feared how powerful my mind was and I felt I had no control over my thoughts. I had attempted suicide at twenty, taking an overdose of prescribed medication. The feeling of not being here anymore seemed to be the only way out. I felt it was the only escape from all the negative crippling thoughts that were in my head. There were so many times throughout the years that I thought of ways to take my own life, I even visualised taking my own life, and right in that moment of visualising I could feel an inner feeling of complete freeness, but a very faint voice in my head would say to me 'You can't leave your children, you can't leave them in this world without their mum, they need you now and they will need you forever. Don't deprive your children of having a mum.'

I felt trapped, I felt scared and lonely, crippled with anxiety, depression and panic attacks that would make me feel as though I was choking to death. The feelings ruled my life, but I couldn't give in to it, I had to stay strong, if not for me for my children. I went through the motions. I took them to school with the biggest of false smiles. I said the happy 'Good morning' or 'Hi' to the other mums and dads. I couldn't show people I was struggling with life. I felt I needed to hide what was going on from the whole world. I even hid it from my family. This was my battle, a battle I needed to fight and a battle I needed to win. I was ashamed of my depression and life's struggles. The self-harming only lasted for a short while as my arms were visible for people to see. I felt the cutting would show people a sign of me being weak, so I found new ways to control myself. I would make myself sick after eating and I would take laxatives so I wouldn't gain weight. It was as if I became obsessive about each thing my mind thought of. If a thought was powerful enough and it was a way of me punishing myself for not being good enough, it would become an obsession.

But after struggling with my mental health for 14 years, I eventually decided not to let it beat me, and now I deal with my mental health in a much healthier way. Although I still slip occasionally, I have learnt over the years how to get myself out of the hole, quicker than I ever was able to in the past. I had years of counselling and CBT (Cognitive Behaviour Therapy) courses, and I self-funded an NLP (Neuro Linguistic Programming) course to help me understand the brain and how it is wired. I needed to learn that I could control my thoughts, my feelings and my actions, that I was in full control of them, not them in control of me. In fact, I now understand that we are all in control of our own thoughts. Just take a few moments to listen to what your thoughts are saying to you. If they are negative, you need to change them in the moment, acknowledging that they are just thoughts. If you struggle emotionally, make a promise to yourself that you are going to change any negative thoughts and you will eventually become happier within yourself. This does take time and a lot of self-awareness but when you start to master your thoughts you really will start to see huge shifts in your life, as I have done. I have listened to hours of inspiring podcast's by Tony Robbins and many other hugely inspiring people, I also have read so many books that have helped me change my view of myself and the world. I no longer live my life as though I am a victim. I am in control of my thoughts and actions. You can be too. By doing the inner work of self-development I know I have made great steps with my mental health and what's more, my family have seen this massive transformation. I would like to share the following six things that helped me hugely.

1. Self-Awareness

Stop yourself right at that moment where your thoughts are talking to you. Listen to what your thoughts are saying to you. If they are negative, you need to change them. This will then change the way you feel and in turn this will change the action you take. Set yourself a new powerful mantra and say it to yourself every day, several times a day, until you believe it. Write your mantra here if you like.

____

____

____

____

____

2. Set yourself a vision

Create a vision board, a group of pictures that represent what you want in life. My vision board is taped tightly inside my wardrobe doors. I get dressed every single day, so my vision is there, in my face reminding me of *why* I am doing what I do now. Create a new vision board each year and push yourself so you can achieve the things you want or come so close to them, a vision that will keep you going until you have achieved them.

3. Question if your circle raises you up or drags you down.

They say you are a result of the five people you spend most time with. Choose the people in your circle wisely, and don't be afraid to let go of the people who don't raise you up. When was the last time you evaluated the people in your circle? Now might be a great time to do this.

4. Mindfulness

Take time out to practice mindfulness and enjoy finding your inner peace. It can take time to get used to the feeling of mindfulness but keep practicing, the results can be life changing for you, as they have for me.

5. Journaling

Write down five positive things every day, even the small stuff, and reflect on all the positives from each day. Don't focus on the negatives. What five things can you think of right now?

____

____

____

____

____

6. Social media scrolling

Have you sat there looking at social media notifications, an hour has passed by before you even know it? Turn off social media activity one hour before bed and one hour after waking. Don't let your mind become consumed by other people's lives. Focus on your life to get the best life for yourself.

Practicing the above daily has allowed me to move through all my life's challenges and pave a better way for myself. I am now happier, stronger and more determined than ever, not only to succeed in life but to help others who are facing struggles overcome them and become more stronger within themselves.

I once had a burning desire so hot and fierce in my belly to be my own boss, to design my own path in life. And now I am. I began thinking about how I could make my dreams a reality instead of lingering on my "failings". I wanted to prove to myself and to other people that I was more than just a teen mum on benefits. I wanted to prove that just because I had an education that pretty much failed, I could still make something of my life. I could still be successful, despite all my setbacks and challenges. With so much self-disbelief, no GCSEs and only a career in care, I wondered what I could do to make my dreams come true!

Then one day whilst doing the weekly household chores, with the music on, I was feeling positive. BOOM! My business idea exploded in my mind! I felt a buzz of excitement. It was an amazing feeling. I remember telling close family members what my idea was. I was going to be a local household name that everyone would know.

I was going to iron people's clothes, but better still I was going to make it as easy as possible for my customers. I was going to offer collection and delivery. My mind started to go off in all directions just like a Sat Nav that's driving you around spaghetti junction. If you don't know Spaghetti junction make a note and check it out. That's what my brain was like! As quick as the excitement came, the feeling of failure came back and smacked me in the face. People told me I was crazy to think about setting up my own business, some even laughed at me, so the doubt crept in. After all, how could it be a success based on my life? Besides, the country was in recession. People told me that it would never work. As a result, I believed them, I doubted myself just as much as they did, and months passed with not one step of action taken to make it all a reality. I procrastinated daily, but with my back to the wall financially, I told myself that '*I MUST DO IT, I CAN DO IT AND I WILL DO IT.*' I had to believe in myself for once, take the risk and prove myself and others wrong.

I called my Dad (again) and asked him if he would lend me some money. He agreed. I found a van, spoke to the seller and when Ashley (my now husband) arrived home from work, I excitedly told him not to take his shoes off, that it was happening, I had the money, I had spoken to a guy who was selling a van and we were going to pick it up. On our way to meet him, I told Ashley that for the first time ever I believed I could do this. I had been thinking about it for six months, with not one ounce of action taken. This was the start of me taking action. I had let the negativity of others control my thoughts, which resulted in me taking no action. This was something that I truly felt would work and something that I could turn into a success.

It was 8pm on a cold December night, and after checking the van (in the pitch-black of night) I agreed to buy it. For the first time in my life I felt proud of myself, still no clue of what lay ahead, but proud that I had taken action and taken my first business risk.

The next morning, on my way to provide my day job caring, I thought about the fact that I had bought a van, an iron and an ironing board from the money that was left over, and I came up with my business name, *The Iron Lady,* with thanks to my dad. I was ready to go, full steam ahead. Only one thing was stopping me — I had no customers! Oh wait, I now needed to market my business, but I had no spare money left at all, no marketing experience, and back in 2008 social media wasn't as advanced as it is today. I went to my local corner shop and asked if I could advertise my ironing service. The shop owner agreed and said that it would be 50p for a two-week Ad. I scrambled the change together out of the drink's holder in my new van, counting all the 5ps and pennies. I took a small piece of cardboard and nervously wrote "Ironing service offered. Collection and delivery available. Please call*** £12.00 a black bag."

I nervously waited and it wasn't very long before the phone rang. It was a lady named Rachel. 'Do you have availability to do some ironing for me?' she said. 'Yes', I said. I tried not to give away how excited I felt over the phone. Having agreed the service, I put the phone down. I was ecstatic. My very first customer, my very first customer that's going to pay me! I was beaming with pride inside. I honestly felt amazing.

Then the phone rang for a second time, another enquiry about my ironing service from the same 50p advert I had put in the shop. I became busier, more and more people were demanding my ironing service, and within four months of setting up my business, I was in a position to hand in my resignation to the care company. Leaving a steady job, one that was guaranteed to bring in an income each month, was another huge risk. *What happens if suddenly I lose all my customers? How would I pay my rent and bills?* However, resigning would mean I could give my new venture my full commitment to growing my client base. I could be my own boss. I thought to myself, *what's the worse than can happen? If it fails, I could go looking for another secure job.* As scary as that may sound, if you are currently in a similar situation ask yourself the question, 'What is the worst that could possibly happen?' And make your decision based on your answer.

I was self-employed with my loyal customer list, which was growing by the day. I was being referred to new people from my existing happy customers. It was a great feeling to be busy and people being happy with my ironing service. Growing to the number of clients I did within the first two years was a huge achievement. I was making more money in a week ironing, than I was caring. Okay, I worked much longer hours every day, but I kept telling myself it will all be worth it one day. It wouldn't just happen, I had to make it happen, and with the support from Ashley, we went out posting leaflets in the freezing cold, on wet rainy days. Ashley really was a huge help when setting up my business, he would come home from a full day's work in his previous job, help load up the van of freshly ironed clothes and deliver them to my clients in the evening; this was a huge help as it allowed me to carry on with the piles of ironing.

I made many sacrifices. I got up at 5am, usually feeling achy and stiff from yesterday's shift, made a cup of piping hot tea whilst I waited for my small domestic iron to heat up, and completed a full bag of ironing before my kids had even woken up. I would take the children to school, spend my full day ironing, collecting freshly washed bags of clothes, doing my drop-offs, then rushing back to collect the children from school. The daily routine after school was very much the same — home, tea, playing games and doing lots of fun things or occasionally we would go out and do something fun, like swimming, a visit to a play centres or just walking up a mountain. Once they were in bed, I would spend hours ironing, sometimes until 2am, only to start all over again at 5am. My evening routine was so different compared to the previous years, my time was consumed with something I was hugely passionate about and thoroughly enjoyed. Knowing this was all for a better life for me and my children made every long hard hour worth it.

I wanted to make sure my customers were happy so they would use my services again and again. I spent extra time making sure their clothes were delivered to them immaculately ironed. Ashley would offer a hand with ironing on the busiest of days, but he was only ever allowed to iron the easy tops and pjs! I hung their clothes, so they were colour coded, from t-shirts to jumpers, neatly hung one by one and all in the correct family member pile, covered in clear bags all labelled up. As long, exhausting and body aching the working hours were, I knew that the only way I was ever going to achieve my dreams and live the future that was stamped in my mind was by making so many sacrifices, there and then.

I reinvested my earnings so I could afford the best ironing systems, I went from a seventy-pound iron in my first year to a three-thousand-pound ironing system in my second year. My home was full of labelled black bags, all piled up waiting to be ironed, and a constant flow of freshly hung clothes waiting to go back. My life and home were taken over, so I decided to reinvest in a lovely large log cabin for the bottom of my garden. This allowed me, the children and Ashley to have our home back and most importantly for Ashley and the kids, as they got our sofa back and work was now out of the house.

The more my ironing customers grew, the more requests I had about doing domestic house cleaning. This was a completely new challenge, but one that I dived head-first into. I quickly learnt the ropes of professional cleaning. Having listened to customers' feedback and having spent hours, weeks and months researching, I felt I had it all nailed. I could clean a home to the highest of standard, whizzing around, polishing, cleaning, buffing and shining the silver, knowing my customers were going to be happy returning home, time and time again.

My business really took off and I could see it was going to go places. In 2010 with the country still in recession, Ashley decided to join my ever-growing business and since then, we have grown it together to be even more successful than my dreams all those years ago.

It would take a full book in itself to share all my stories, adventures and learnings from my twelve years in business with my husband, building an amazing team, leading a team, dealing with the daily challenges a business owner faces, etc. but I would like to share with you the ten nuggets that made my business what it is today. You might like to apply these to your dreams.

- Never give up when times get tough.
- Be prepared to make huge sacrifices and work the long hours in the early years.
- Be prepared to take risks.
- Don't be afraid of failing.
- Build a strong team around you.
- Employ people who are better than you. Know your strengths and your weaknesses.
- Look after and reward your team.
- Look after your customers.
- Trust your intuition.
- Create processes that makes your business so robust, even in a crisis you are prepared.

At the time of writing I am married nearly ten years to my wonderful husband and business partner Ashley. My children are now in their middle and late teens, and in the past 12 months I am happier than I have ever been in my life. We have two-hundred-plus employees, a work culture that is one we are very proud of, a team that has always got ours back 100%, and our business has just turned over a staggering £2 million pounds in the last twelve months. We have won some incredible business awards over the years and we have so many plans to continue the businesses growth and to keep developing our amazing, hardworking, loyal team around us, a team that is as passionate as we are about providing our services to our customers and to promote our people's development. We have a client portfolio that has taken years to develop, by building strong relationships, a portfolio that we are very proud of. With commitment, huge sacrifices, and dedication, the seemingly impossible has become possible.

With all of the above going on in my life daily, I also pushed myself outside of my comfort zone in other ways, signing myself up to do some crazy challenges. I completed a trek in the Patagonia Mountains, I did a 600K charity bike ride, I ran the 2019 London Marathon for a mental health charity, which was a whopping 26.2 miles, I skydived for charity, amongst many other challenges for charity. To date I have raised over £35k for various charities. So, no matter what your life is currently like, no matter how big a challenge may appear, break it down into bite-size manageable pieces and watch yourself overcome challenge after challenge, and achieve goal after goal. Keep raising your bar, push your boundaries and keep striving to be the happiest you can be each day of your life, regardless of any negative thoughts or fears. You can reach your dreams, just believe in yourself!

My lasting message to you is to never be afraid to step out of your comfort zone. If you do the same thing day in, day out, you will only achieve the same results you are currently achieving. You can harness the feeling of fear and turn it into your best asset. It isn't easy (it's not meant to be easy) but after every challenge you overcome, you will become stronger. Learn from your mistakes, set yourself a vision, a vision that even on the toughest of days makes you get out of bed and do all that's needed so you can, one day, live your life like you once dreamed of. Believe in yourself every single day. Make sure the words you tell yourself are words that lift you up, not beat you down.

You can live your absolute best life, if you are prepared to take the risks, make the sacrifices and never give up. You may need to take a different direction to get to your end goal but if you believe in your goals, you can beat all the odds that are against you right now. I hope my journey has left you feeling that you can do absolutely anything you put your mind to, you just need to want it. Learn from every event that knocks you down, let it build up your resilience, and learn to get back up quicker. Remember, one thing if nothing else from my journey, no matter how tough times may be, NEVER GIVE UP! If I can do it, then you absolutely can! Embrace the caterpillar and become the butterfly!

Design your Destiny
by Liz Hickey

Do you believe in destiny? In miracles? Even in magic? Well I do. I have had too many examples of these over the years to ignore them. I have also experienced moments of true destiny. You know when you are there. It is a certain feeling of synchronicity, of all being well in your world, and kind of 'meant to be.'

On turning 60, one of my wishes was to be an author, hence my involvement in writing this book with this wonderful group of women under Donna's mentoring and as with so many other things in my life, I found a way to make it happen, even when it seemed impossible. I set an intention. It took a year. It actually felt like I had waved a magic wand. I have felt this feeling of magical synchronicity many times myself, but also when rearing my family or working with others.

It is only in recent times I have discovered that I am what is known as an HSP (a Highly Sensitive Person) and this explains so much. Since childhood all my senses have been heightened. I can feel other people's emotions and energy and kind of read their thoughts. I have had to find ways to manage my highly sensitive nature, as negative situations can be overwhelming, and people's words can hurt me deeply. I recognised this since early childhood. I only understand it from my work with a wonderful healer, for about 2 years now.

On the other hand, this sensitivity can be a superpower too, allowing me to have great insight in situations and more recently, helping people to understand what they really want, love and enjoy in life.

Life's Compensations

I understand now that I received compensations to help me deal with this extreme sensitivity. Firstly, my creativity, flair for colour and talent for designing and making things. Secondly, my ability to ideate and come up with a wealth of ideas. Thirdly, my wonderful zest for life – a powerful wish to live life to the full, and on my terms, through different life situations.

A further compensation is that I met the love of my life, Philip, at 19 and he has walked life's journey with me for over 40 years now through ups and downs and amazing moments too.

My life experience and recent studies have resulted in the creation of 'Lifedesign', a process that I was given the seeds of as a child and that I have nurtured, developed and used repeatedly for myself and others. I now know that Lifedesign is the main life skill that has helped me to survive and thrive in life and I have used it to rear my family, build our relationship and to help many other people along the way too.

I have now found a way to teach Lifedesign and to teach other people how to teach it too. Anyone can use it, if they wish, to design aspects of their life to make life better for themselves in all kinds of ways. Lifedesign can help us to get out of tricky life situations and create solutions. It can also help us to get what we really want and need in life, rather than settling for what life throws at us. It helps us design occasions and even moments and can make the mundane more interesting and life more enjoyable in all kinds of ways. When the time is right, it can help us make our difference in the world.

The Journey of Life

We arrive in this world, landing with parent/s and perhaps siblings. They say we choose our family. I'm sure many would disagree. I have been truly lucky with mine. Depending on our culture, we humans have to fit into all kinds of traditions, reach milestones and fulfil many expectations of family and society.

To be 'different' in life, or regarded as 'different', whether by your sensitivity, the colour of your skin, your culture, your sexuality, your life circumstances, your level of ability or the size of your body, can be a lifelong challenge. I have always been 'different', and this has given me a huge understanding of human nature, from kindness to cruelty and back to kindness. In my experience, it takes courage and creativity and hope to survive and thrive. This is where Lifedesign has really helped me personally.

As a parent, I believe that children need to learn life skills beyond what is taught in normal family life and school. The needs of a shy child or an outgoing child or a sensitive child are completely different. I would suggest that the greatest gift we can give our children is to teach them to be aware of their own needs and to find ways to fulfil these that are positive and affirming. Otherwise, they may not be equipped with the skills they need to deal with everything from an impatient teacher, to the challenges of the playground, to learning difficulties they may encounter, almost inevitable bullying and even little disappointments along the way. Some of these childhood experiences are the root of many adult woes.

Even the youngest children can be taught basic Lifedesign skills. If a child has a problem, if they learn to dig deep creatively, they will often have the solution. In fact, in my own experience of mothering, if you sit down with even a young child experiencing a problem and ask gentle questions, they will often have the solution too and this is really empowering for them. When you work out the solutions together and make a little plan, it is a lovely addition to the bond of love and trust you share, that can go on into teenage years.

Sometimes I dream of a country that understands human needs and ensures they are fulfilled for most of their citizens, whatever their age or difference and there are certainly countries that we can take example from. I wish for a country where life skills are as important as reading and writing.

About Lifeskills

We often learn life skills from family members. You might be a great baker as you watched your mother or grandmother bake bread. You might be good at carpentry or DIY because you followed your father around the house. You might love gardening, because you watched someone plant flower or vegetable seeds, as I did. My ability to knit came from a teacher who loved knitting. But I know for sure, it is possible to learn life skills at every stage in life and it is wonderful to see that many primary schools have school gardens now where children can experience the cycles of the seasons and see where food actually comes from.

I have many what I call 'Lifedesign stories' to tell, but I will start with one when I was fifteen. I just knew there was more to life than kind of hanging around with friends. I really liked people and wanted to find a way to earn some money and help people. I had been doing this since childhood. I had babysitting jobs I really enjoyed but I wanted more. I remember going around the town where I lived, on my bike, looking at all the different shops and businesses, from clothes shops to knitting shops to chippers, butchers and bakeries wondering how I could get make life more interesting. Could I get a job?

I was literally drawn to a certain pharmacy. The bell rang as I went in the door. It was dark and a mixture of smells. A lady in a white coat came out from the back and stood behind the counter. I told her my name and said that I was looking for a Saturday job. She took off her glasses and smiled at me and asked me my age. She smiled at me again and said that she could do with an assistant to dust the display cabinets and give her a general helping hand. Spotting my bike, she said 'you could also deliver parcels to our older or very sick customers'. I remember being delighted. I had done it! I had a job. I had turned an idea into something great. It was a real sense of achievement. I knew this job would bring me freedom. What I didn't realize was that I had signed up for an 'apprenticeship' of sorts that lasted ten years of Saturdays and school holidays and I learned a huge amount of medical information and people skills that would be so useful at a later stage in life.

I quickly learned the personalities, family situations, problems and woes of many of the customers. I could often offer them solutions. From time to time I noticed the owner of the pharmacy smiling as I offered a suggestion beyond my years and certainly beyond the norm. Sometimes these suggestions seemed to come into my head from some other source! Eventually a few customers used to ask for me on Saturdays to have a chat. I found myself advising on make-up shades and lipstick colours before I had even started wearing them myself. I later found myself listening to stories and being told things in confidence. I realised quickly that the height of the counter protected me from taking on their sadness or troubles. I thought everyone needed this protection and that was why it was so high.

Those ten years taught me so much. The owner of the pharmacy was a medical doctor and she just loved imparting knowledge to me. She told me stories about being a female doctor when there were few, of delivering babies in the tenements in Dublin, of the importance of treating everyone as equals. She told me stories of working in London, of knowing our values and the importance of family loyalty. She taught me names and uses of medicines that I still use today. She showed me how to spot infections, dress wounds and to find ways to help those less well off.

I learned skills in this little job, that have helped me so much in life. The doctor also sowed seeds in my mind of all that was possible. I am very grateful for this. Our teachers can come into our lives in all different ways. My mother told me recently that it was this doctor's wish that I take over her business, but that was not my destiny.

Are there life skills you have that you feel really help you in life? Let's take a moment to write them down:

1. ____
2. ____
3. ____
4. ____
5. ____

From time to time it is nice to think about ourselves and where we are at now in life, as reviewing the skills we have can often help us identify gaps, which can then be filled through education, whether watching videos on the topic, or taking a course online or offline.

Are there dreams you have and wishes to be fulfilled in your life? It could be finding love, or a dream job, or having a longed-for baby or a more comfortable place to live or even setting up a business that would bring more income and therefore more possibilities. These might be things that you haven't got around to yet for all kinds of reasons. If so, write them here, because acknowledging these and writing them down, is like writing a wish-list or placing an order with the Universe.

1. ______________________________
2. ______________________________
3. ______________________________
4. ______________________________
5. ______________________________

Keep going and add more if you wish dear reader – there are no limits – and you may be surprised that at least one of them might feel even a little more achievable, when I tell you more Lifedesign stories.

Zest for life

Jumping ahead, when I left school, having failed maths, I could not study pharmacy as I had hoped, in fact the doors of banks, insurance companies and other employers were closed to me too. I worked for many years in a company where I felt bullied and I feared my personality and creativity might be snuffed out, so I began to demonstrate my organisational skills and colour skills and they quickly picked up on them and began to use them. I found myself really interested in colour and interiors and found ways to study these when they were not available here in Ireland.

I was always finding solutions, for myself and for others. As I mentioned earlier, my deep sensitivity allowed me to be really empathetic to their needs.

I lived with my eyes wide open. I loved meeting people from other countries and learning about their cultures. My father travelled the world and he would bring back all kinds of tales and send me a postcard from every destination, which opened my mind to a world way beyond 1970s Ireland. He also invited people of many nationalities to visit us.

I used my ideation skills to live all kinds of experiences. By the time I was 19 I had been on several foreign holidays. My mind was full of hopes and dreams and wishes for myself, but for others and even for society too. It's like I could always see a bigger picture. Different life experiences, people I met through my parents, houses I visited, places I went fuelled my imagination for what is possible in life. I knew at an early age I didn't like the pub culture here in Ireland and wondered how I would ever find a partner who had the same values, vision and energy as I had and match my zest for life.

Lifedesign Manifestation

I had a way of making things happen, like a personal manifestation skill, though I knew nothing of such things. My

Mum often referred to it as luck. I would think up what for some might be a crazy idea (certainly in the 70's and 80's). I might figure it out in my head and in my dreams. For something bigger or more complicated, I would write it down and surround it with notes, ideas, possibilities, perhaps people's names, things I would have to do make it happen. I preferred to do this in colour. Then I would find a starting point and put all the pieces together like a jigsaw puzzle until what I wished for materialised, like magic! I didn't know this way of creating things was pretty unique to me. It was an early version of what I now call 'Lifedesign'.

In more recent years, when the going was tough, I thought I had lost my magic touch – but looking back, I realise that Lifedesign has always seen me through.

Lifedesign and My Relationship

I had booked a holiday with a friend and in the meantime used to go to a folk mass in a church that was not my parish. I liked the vibe of the young group of people so I asked the priest if I could join the folk group. I was looking for my tribe! His initial answer was 'no because I was not a parishioner', but like the pharmacy owner he looked at me and saw 'something' and told me to come back in a couple of weeks and he would think about it. I went off on holidays.

I remember on the plane home wondering how I was going to make the time between now and my next holiday really good. At this stage I had three jobs (including Saturdays in the pharmacy and two evenings a week in a fine dining restaurant where I met all kinds of interesting people). I remember thinking I was going to find all kinds of new ways to add to my list of friends and to interact with even more interesting people (really setting goals before anyone spoke about goal setting though I like to think of them as hopes, dreams and wishes).

After mass the next day, the priest called me over and invited me to join the folk group. I was delighted. The next evening, I went to a practice with the group. A guy asked me to go to a party on the Saturday night. On the evening of the party, he said he did not feel like going and I said, 'well drop me off at the party – I want to meet everyone in the folk group'. I always had a mind of my own.

House parties were all the rage. I found myself sitting on a sofa between the priest and Philip. Philip walked me home, I was just so comfortable in his company. Six weeks later, the folk group went to the West to stay in a wonderful house. The priest came as a chaperone. Philip and I sneaked away from the group to sleep by the fire, innocently, in this amazing old house. Our priest friend came in and just smiled at us. The next morning, we went for a walk by a lake. When we sat down, Philip asked me to marry him. We were both nineteen. The priest noticed us from the other side of the lake. He could see we were in love. He came over and gave us this beautiful blessing that I believe has lived on with us. A magical experience. This wonderful priest eventually married us, christened our three children and buried my Dad. He is still our friend, though the Catholic church holds little interest for me now, yet I respect all religions.

I honestly believe I Lifedesigned this relationship of ours and then the Gods intervened to make it happen... Philip quickly became a Lifedesigner too. I really believe, that to live a wonderful life, we have to dream big, get really clear on what we love and enjoy and then life will align to make amazing things happen, if they are our destiny.

Early Lifedesign Skills

Our long relationship has been designed through some very difficult and sad times and through wonderful experiences too. We constantly set intentions and followed through on them. Our wedding was designed and was way ahead of its time in many ways. I remember deciding I wanted drop pearls for my dress and a scalloped veil and on a whim, went to find them in London. Now this was 1980! We took the 'Magic Bus' from Dun Laoghaire, which went on the ferry, drove through the night and delivered us in London at 5am. We got on the 'Magic Bus' again that evening with the pearls, a veil bought in Harrods and a set of cutlery from Habitat, long before the store was in Ireland.

Our little place to live was designed and could have been photographed for a magazine. What do I mean by designed? I mean thought through and created with flair, for comfort and practicality, but just a touch of extravagance too.

In a designed life, we can stretch ourselves beyond boundaries we do not believe in. We can bring people into our lives to inspire us. Having creativity in our lives helps us see opportunities and follow through. It helps us think beyond the obvious. Someone said to me recently, 'but design is about art and graphics and products.' I confidently said, 'it is also about life'. I know this to be true. We have honestly, designed our way into and out of so many different things.

Lifedesigning Our Family

In September 1990, we went away for our wedding anniversary, a little tradition we had put in place. While staying in a lovely country house, we saw in the newspapers the plight of the children in Romania. I said to Philip, kind of flippantly, how I would love to adopt one of these children to start our family. He agreed with me that it would be wonderful. I won't go into great detail here, but this was all the encouragement I needed. It took me 6 weeks to get in contact with couples who had adopted children, to find out what was possible and how to proceed. This was long before we were using the internet and mobile phones!

I remember sitting down and 'designing' a set of documents I thought might be acceptable to the authorities in Romania, based on my research, and the authorities here when I returned. My years in the office job I disliked, had taught me excellent admin skills and most of all tenacity. Often, I have found, life is preparing us for what our next calling will be. I had the name of one person in Romania who said to call them if we went there. We headed off on 27 November 1990 and to cut a long story short, I arrived home on 13 December 1990 with our wonderful son, Andrew. This trip was like a whirlwind and probably deserves its own book.

Andrew had suffered greatly and was very unwell and malnourished. Nobody here could really tell me what to do to bring him to full health. I had to use every ounce of my common sense, my knowledge from the pharmacy, my years of babysitting, my intuition and most of all my creativity to do this. Moving on three years, having learned that we would not have our own children, in 1994 and 1996 we adopted our wonderful daughters, Sophie and Rachel. Each adoption took great tenacity and creative thinking and a lot of heartache to make happen. It is my greatest joy to be their mum. I have no doubt that we succeeded because of Lifedesign.

You remember I mentioned destiny? Well the way our family was created is an example of pure destiny. Your destiny does not always arrive on your doorstep or fall into your lap – you have got to step towards it with conviction and then hand things over to a Higher Power, or the Universe, whatever your faith, or none.

What I learned from this whole experience, and it flows into my Lifedesign process, is to get really clear and set an intention, whether big or small and then step towards it and put it together, like you would build a jigsaw, piece by piece. I also learned that you cannot do it all alone. If it were not for my wonderful friend in Romania, we would be childless.

Lifedesigning Our Way Through Challenges

Over the years, my dear Dad had several very serious illnesses and I remember, with my Mum, brother and sister, putting on our thinking caps and helping him design his way back to health several times. On one occasion, he was on life support for 12 weeks and had to learn to walk again. On another occasion, he had leukaemia and again it was a long journey back to reasonable health. Sadly, he died in 2013 and we all miss him greatly. We were truly lucky that he was with us for those extra years, long enough for our kids to get to know and love him.

Perhaps you know the feeling when the bottom falls out of your world? In December 2004, I was standing on the top floor of a city centre shop car park, when I received a call from Philip to say our business was gone. We had designed a life that required his high earnings and I worked for the company too at that stage. Both of us found ourselves queuing in the Social Welfare office, just weeks before Christmas. This business was a huge loss both to us and to the many companies who benefitted from its financial service. I was deeply worried, but I knew that with our lifedesign skills, we would get through, somehow. I often think now that we suffered a personal recession, before the global recession and we still live with some of the consequences.

The years between 2004 and 2009, were very difficult for us. It really took every bit of creativity and tenacity we could muster to keep ourselves afloat. We lost a holiday home and were constantly pursued by Vulture Funds. We withstood 7 years of unemployment and had to accept help of all kinds. Every time we reached the edge, we would brainstorm and get through. We honestly designed our way through.

I continued studies I had started in NLP and other healing techniques. I quickly realised that I was far too sensitive for this work, listening to people's troubles and problems was not for me. I decided I would like to become a stylist and literally that week, saw an advertisement offering to train style coaches — more magic! I got a grant towards this training as I could not have afforded it. I set up a small business to fit in with fulltime motherhood. I loved the work. It kept me stimulated and creative and I loved helping people to look good and feel great, whatever their age or their size or their life challenges. I worked with people 1-1, but I also ran courses and offered shopping and decluttering services. In 2009, with the dawn of the recession, the phone stopped ringing. My little business was all but gone.

A bird with a broken wing

In 2009, several projects Philip had been working on disappeared and as he was at home, searching for work, he could do school drop offs and pick-ups and generally care for the kids, I decided to go to back into education. Having failed maths, college had not been a possibility when I left school. I started at Level 5, then I was deflated when I was turned down for art college, but I thought creatively about my possibilities and applied for a Level 7 degree in Business and Entrepreneurship. I started in IADT, Dun Laoghaire, aged 51, feeling like a bird with a broken wing. I was emotionally drained by all that had befallen us and as a HSP (Highly Sensitive Person). I was very sad to see what was happening to so many people in Ireland and to experience all we had worked for threatened and friendships falling by the wayside. Our son was a year ahead of me at the college but was happy for me to be there too. Our kids have been extremely understanding and helpful through our many years of challenges. At times, it felt like we would lose everything, yet we have lost nothing. We have certainly struggled and been stretched to the limit, but we have survived and in our own simple way, thrived as a family and are grateful for so many helping hands along the way.

I thought I would just go to college for one year and the recession would be over. However, I stayed three years and graduated with a Level 7 degree with Distinction and a special award from the college. During this time, I decided to set up a social enterprise called Step up Ireland. On the Facebook page, I encouraged people to design their lives rather than settle for what had happened to them in the recession – it is still active with a large following and I still share creative ideas for business and life there. It now forms part of my Lifedesign plans.

I loved academic life. I loved learning. I loved the comradeship. We are so lucky in Ireland that education is so readily available to us. I had the opportunity to complete my Level 8 degree on a Springboard course. I then went to the Innovation Academy in UCD where I discovered a topic called 'Design Thinking' as taught at Harvard. I was hooked. I wanted to know more. Design

Thinking described perfectly the kind of brainstorming and blue sky thinking I had always done as part of Lifedesign. I had something to hang my own concept on. It was amazing. I continued to Trinity College to do a further course on this topic and studied innovation too.

As I considered Lifedesign and how I would bring it to the world, I then decided to study Digital Marketing, returning to my original college part-time, again on a Springboard course. At this stage, these post grad studies formed two thirds of a master's degree. I took a deep breath and jumped in and finished it, graduating November 2018, on the same day as my daughter Rachel received her degree in English, Media and Cultural Studies.

In the meantime, Sophie had studied Business and Entrepreneurship too. In fact, I spent time in college with all three of my kids. Andrew had studied Business & Event Management and working at events he discovered his passion for paramedic work. Having taken an EMT course and volunteering, he then transferred to working in that field and being a true lifedesigner, he is currently working as a trainee paramedic on blue lights ambulances in the UK and has just started a BSc course in Paramedic Practice – Remote Hazardous Environments.

Studying at the same time as my kids gave me great insight into the complexities of transitioning from secondary school to college, the pressures of college on our young people and insight into the life of millennials. The transition from college to working life can be equally complicated. Knowing exactly what to do with your degree benefits greatly from lifedesign skills too. Rachel will, two years later, return to college to study a M.Ed., in order to teach.

I should add that any learning challenges or bullying the kids encountered in their school years were dealt with using our Lifedesign process. Philip was so incredibly supportive all along the way and I am very grateful for this.

Lifelong Learning

Have you ever considered returning to learning? Or do you by any chance have a wish to return to education of any kind? If so, I would strongly encourage you to do so. There are so many different routes and so much support along the way and you will find a way through. I leave a space here for you to make a note about this if you wish, because, there is no doubt in my mind that what we write down, we can make happen and that all manner of helping hands come our way.

____

____

____

____

Lifelong learning allows us to grow, reinvent and become all we can be in the world. It builds confidence and self-belief and there is so much support along the way in our colleges, whether with literary skills, dyslexia, dyspraxia or anything else that may arise. Online learning using well researched courses is very empowering and to this day, I continue my learning with courses in the USA and Holland. With the internet, there are no limits.

Your Vision for You

Learning happens in all kinds of ways; I am sure you will agree. Many people refer to the fact that they have been to 'life school' and I certainly have been too. One way to get clear on what you really want in life, is to spend time either observing, or with people who live, think and act in ways you would like to emulate.

Often in the context of my work, I am shocked at how small people's vision for themselves is. You see, even one disappointment can stop us in our tracks or keep us stuck. I love opening people's minds to their possibilities and then they choose what they would like to do/achieve. They are always in the driving seat

Pausing for a moment, if you believed that you wouldn't fail — is there something that you would just love to achieve in your life? Because with the right support and Lifedesign skills, it truly is possible. I have seen it so many times. Make a little note here, it's like sowing a magic seed.

____

____

____

I believe that everyone has a deep wisdom and knows what they truly want, but sometimes this gets covered up by life experiences. When I pull back the cover slightly and help people find a starting point, or look at their situation from another perspective, their whole facial expression changes to one of possibility. I love this part of my work.

Please realise that it is never too late to do something you would really like to do. Every new day you have the opportunity to point yourself towards your destiny. Lifedesign will certainly get you there, but more importantly, it will help you to enjoy each day and week on the way there too. It really is a way of living.

The Power of Creativity

Research shows that everyone is inherently creative, but that although creativity is included in the primary school curriculum, much of this creativity is lost in the secondary school system. As a child, I went to a Montessori school until I was 12, so secondary school was a real challenge for me. If it was not for the refuge of the art room and the library, I am not sure how this highly sensitive child would have got through those years.

As we know, in our society, reading, writing and maths are the route to further education, if you are lucky to get there through life's obstacles, including where you land in the world. We humans, I believe, need our creativity to play the 'game of life'. Employers now look for qualities such as innovation, creativity and people skills. The education system has to catch up with this.

Once inherent creativity has been lost along the way, can it be regained? Without it, how do we have the means to be entrepreneurs or broad thinking politicians or teachers that capture the children's attention day in and day out and find ways to teach the challenged child? Most importantly, without creativity how do we get ourselves out of a difficult situation? How do we imagine new ways of doing things? I would even ask how on earth do we survive and thrive?

What we need to realise is that there are hundreds of ways to bring creativity into our lives and to acknowledge these, whether it is planting a pot in our garden, choosing the clothes we wear or picking a paint colour for a room.

Having worked as an interior designer many moons ago, I was often surprised that by the end of a project, people who had said in the beginning that they hadn't a clue what they wanted or what colours worked together, had a well-informed opinion about both.

Sometimes we have to be given permission to unleash our creativity. Perhaps this is because life has not given us opportunities to do this, or perhaps it is because of some life experience such as lack of praise for a piece of art as a child, or that a friend who seemed better at colouring than you, deflated your opinion of your creativity.

Sometimes when working with a client, I give them basic creative materials, colouring pencils, a design to colour, little images, colours to arrange in shades, or even invite them to doodle as we chat. I watch as their faces relax, and often notice that their need to be perfect eases. This experience gives them time out they need to figure things out, connected with the creative side of their brain.

I know from my studies that creative skills can be learned at any stage of life, but also that these skills can keep us company right into old age. For example, my lovely Mum who is 86 as I write, gave me permission to mention that she gathers with 8 other women around her kitchen table on Monday afternoons and they craft and chat and have lovely friendships.

I am not a creativity expert, but I know for sure that creative practice, meaning any hobbies that use our hands and mind, ease anxiety, create a positive mind body connection, and can bring us even a little peace and solace, both day to day and in troubled times. Creativity brings me ease, as an HSP (Highly Sensitive Person). Creativity connects us with and switches on our imagination...

Are there creative skills you have and use?

1. ____
2. ____
3. ____

Are there creative skills you have and might like to use again?

1. ____
2. ____
3. ____

Are there creative skills you would really like to learn?

1. ____
2. ____
3. ____

Imagine if you could unlock your full quota of creativity and begin to use it as a superpower in your life?

Perhaps achieving what you truly want is easier than you might have imagined, with the right information, advice, support and inspiration and being really in tune with your own talents, hopes and dreams. That is what Lifedesign allows to evolve.

Lifedesign as a Lifeskill

In recent years I have helped friends, strangers and more recently, clients, to embrace Lifedesign and the difference it makes is very evident. Because of my experience with it, given a few minutes with anyone, I can help them solve a problem creatively and give them hope. In fact, the most fundamental outcome from using Lifedesign is hope. Yes, we achieve things, we sort things out, but we also gain hope in what is possible.

With Lifedesign we begin to truly acknowledge who we are and what we bring to the world. We acknowledge our skills, talents and abilities. We learn what we like and enjoy and are honest about what we do not like or enjoy in our lives. These may surprise you! We get clear. Really clear. We get creative. We set intentions. We gather and share our resources. We brainstorm like crazy and in really creative ways (it's called blue sky brainstorming). We use aspects of Design Thinking. We make a decision and a five-step plan and most importantly, really, really acknowledge when we achieve something rather than rushing on to the next intention, because the power is in this acknowledgement. And gratitude, we live with gratitude.

It sounds simple, and it is, but once taught in depth to you — and that is why I teach individuals Lifedesign techniques and teach group courses online and offline called 'Lifedesign as a Life skill' — you have a life-changing and life-enhancing skill to use yourself, to teach your family, to pass on to others and a ripple of success begins to grow.

It is important to interact with others who are experimenting with Lifedesign too, as we begin to speak a language of positivity and success. Not forced positivity, rather positivity based in our reality. Whatever is going on in our lives, we can have a Lifedesign project on the go, keeping us up-beat and future-focused and feeling that we are designing our way forward, while really present in and enjoying now, if at all possible. We start with a simple question every time:

Who am I and what do I bring to the world?

____

____

____

____

____

You would be absolutely shocked how many people struggle with this question. Sometimes it just starts with one or two words, and I have experienced this myself at the start of my learning journey in 2004. I just saw myself as a wife and mum and yet I know now I was so much more.

Lifedesign in Action

We thought our troubles were over when Philip started a new business a few years ago. The Gods aligned; the potential was huge. But this was not to be. Commercial circumstances prevent me from sharing a very challenging story. When he told me what had happened, he said 'Liz, plug me into Lifedesign, I need it to get me though this'. This time, I taught him the Lifedesign process I had developed. He will now help me to teach Lifedesign to certain audiences. I now know I will teach others to teach Lifedesign too in a professional capacity, either as an add on to their current offering or a stand-alone business in a box, offering others an entrepreneurial opportunity under the Lifedesign umbrella.

Last year, as at other times in our life, Mr Lifedesign (as I sometimes call him) and myself sat down together on a few occasions, and using the Lifedesign process, created two new seedling businesses. We face the future with optimism and a sense of excitement, despite ongoing challenges.

Philip also lectures at a Dublin College, sharing his expertise with students from all over the world. He is an amazing teacher and mentor in the world of Fintech. I am so excited that he will work with me in The Lifedesign Institute. We have both reinvented several times and it has certainly made life interesting.

In ways, we find ourselves starting all over again. But that is okay. It keeps us pretty youthful and very creative and we trust that after some really difficult life challenges over the years, with some amazing times sprinkled in between, whether rearing our family, growing beautiful flowers in our garden, enjoying stolen moments together, taking our little road trips, or creating family occasions 'we can create our future, based on the foundations of the past' to quote a poem on Motherhood I wrote many years ago.

Designing a new Decade

As we start this new decade, I hope and pray we will both have the health and courage to continue to design our personal and joined destinies and I wish you the opportunity to do likewise. Why? Because it is your precious life. Claim it and live every day to the full!

From my personal experience and my further experience working with others, I truly believe that given reasonable physical and mental health, we can design our way into and out of anything in life, if it is our destiny. We are living proof of this. Our kids are now grown and laughingly calling themselves 'Lifedesigners' as they each forge their own way forward on their unique journeys and bring their lovely partners into our lives. We are so proud of them.

Do get the help and support you need. I invested in this. I would not be where I am today without it. I invested when I could not afford to. I invested when my daughters had to help me do so. I invested when it did not make financial sense, but it did make Lifedesign sense. Discover what help, support and guidance you need and value yourself enough to get it.

Our mission going forward, is to share 'Lifedesign as a Lifeskill' with as many people as possible in Ireland and beyond, building a global community of Lifedesigners, as Philip and I know from personal experience, that it is a pretty phenomenal way of living. I will end my chapter by sharing the quote I live by:

'My mission in life is not merely to survive, but to thrive;
and to do so with some passion, some compassion,
some humour and some style'

\- Maya Angelou

Be the Change
by Katharina Ashlin

I hope that by the end of this short story you will be able to understand how important it is to *'Be the Change'* in your life and learn to implement some things into your life that I have learned. Or allow your awareness to rise and see things with a different light. True changes happened for me back in the 90s when I had my kids and became a parent. My journey into parenthood was an eye opener to the way I grew up. Let me take you back to when I was a kid.

My dad so wanted a daughter and I arrived in 1965, the second and last child to complete the family. I was born at home and my Nan was there when I arrived. We did not have a lot back then, and the house my dad had purchased was a converted barn with no central heating. We had one room with a stove that was used for cooking and heating. The one room was a kitchen/dining and front room in one. Everything happened there.

My brother and I shared a room beside my parent's room. In the winter it was cold, but we had thick bedding, so we did not feel the cold. My mom was always the first one up, lighting the fire and bringing in wood so that we had that one room heated and the window clear of ice crystals in the winter. There were always ice crystals on the window in the winter because of the hard frost. I love these memories as they allow me to reflect on what we have now and how we managed back then with very little.

As kids, we always played outside if it was not raining. We were very healthy, growing up in the countryside. We learned from a very early age how to collect wood in the forest, and once collected, it was chopped, and we had to stack it up to dry. We had two neighbours, one had three kids and the others had none. Town was a thirty-minute walk. My mum did not have a car, only a moped that she used to do the shopping with. My dad was not home much as he worked away. He was home at the weekends and most of the time he was extremely stressed. He was self-employed and had a lot going on with work, making sure we were fed, and taking care of his employees too. When I look back at my childhood, there was a lot of arguing back then. As I grew up, I began to think it was normal. My dad was strict, and we got a smack if we stepped out of line. He got the same treatment when he was a child.

We would listen to the adults telling stories about their past when we could. As kids it was fantastic to listen to the adventures and experiences they had. My Nan was the sweetest of them all. She was kind and I loved her so much. In the summer I often went and stayed with her when, I was allowed.

When I was five years old, I wanted to stay with my Nan, but I was not allowed to. I asked my mum if I could take her bike and cycle around. When she agreed I took the bike out of the chickens' house and off I went to my Nan's house. It was a 12 km cycle on main roads with no cycle lanes. I was scared and stopped every time I heard a lorry coming and moved aside. They looked like monsters to me. I was small and they were so noisy and big. I'm not sure how long it took me to get to my Nan's house, but when I got there she said, 'How did you get here?' When I told her that I had cycled she didn't believe me. Instead she asked me if my dad had dropped me at the bottom of the hill. I told her that I cycled there on my mum's bike. Concerned, she questioned if my parents knew where I was. Of course, I had not told them. My mum just thought I was cycling around the house.

My Nan panicked as she had no phone and no car. She ran to the neighbour's house to call my mum and asked her if she knew where I was. My mum told her that I was cycling around the house with her bike! I think they must have both been relieved, knowing that I was safe, and I was allowed to stay. I was over the moon. I have lots of memories of my childhood.

My mum was always busy. She had me and my brother to look after our massive garden and a big yard. We grew a lot of vegetables and had many different fruit trees. We had chickens, ducks and turkeys, rabbits in a pen, a dog and a few cats. We were surrounded by forest and fields with cows and land.

We helped in the summer with the bales of straw when the farmer harvested the grains. Best of all we built little houses with the straw that was not collected. The neighbour's kids were the same age as us and we had friends up from school in the summer too. My neighbour was mostly in charge and she told me what I could and could not do and whom I could play with. My mum was always too busy with everything. My neighbour sometimes bullied me, but it was overlooked in order to avoid conflict. Confronting my neighbour was not something my mom had time for, and she hadn't the ability to deal with conflict. I didn't really have a choice but to do as I was told.

One summer I was playing in our garden with the girl from next door called Heidi. We started fighting over my skipping rope. We were both pulling at the same time and my leg got caught in it. I screamed and my neighbour did not know what to do. I was screaming in so much pain that my mother came into the garden. As she did, the girl disappeared. A different neighbour who heard me screaming, came into the garden and carried me to the house while my mum ran down the road to the garden centre to get a lift to the hospital. Neither of our neighbours had cars and my dad was away working. So, the only option was to ask the owner of the garden centre if he could take us to the hospital.

After a bumpy and painful ride in the old Beetle, we arrived at the hospital. The X-rays confirmed that my shins were broken, and my leg had to be put in plaster. I had to stay in hospital for two weeks. The plaster went all the way up my leg and I absolutely hated it. But on a positive note, my dad always brought ice cream for all the kids in the ward when he came to visit me.

My granddad collected me the day I was discharged from hospital. We drove by the school on the way home and I told my granddad I wanted to go to that school. However, he said the people there would think I was a monster if they saw me with my leg in cast. I was sad as I wanted to play with all those kids in the school yard.

Back home I could not do much and I couldn't escape Heidi when she came around. She was very persistent. She brought an old pram one day so she could push me around in it. My mum was happy to let her as she was busy and could not attend to me all the time. Sometimes it was fun, but I always had to do what she wanted to do, not what I wanted to do.

As I recovered, I managed to move around and wear the heel of the plaster down in the process. I hated having to have a new one put on. I screamed the first couple of times when they switched on the electric saw to cut the plaster. No matter how much the doctor tried to calm me, I was scared he would cut my leg off. My parents were not in the room to comfort me. They were too busy and stressed making ends meet. They expected me to just grin and bear it. My dad would vent his frustration out on us when he was home. He would tell us to study so we wouldn't end up stupid. As a child I tried to escape many times as I hated the arguing and shouting that went on. I suppose, looking back, my dad carried on the behaviour he learned as he was growing up. As a child, you tend to forget the good times, too. I understand now that my parents had a tough upbringing which they later passed on in their parenting style with us.

My mother's upbringing was tough. She grew up never having met her dad as he died in the war. When Poland claimed land back from Germany my mother's family was torn apart. She had to leave what was once her home to go and live in another part of Germany with her Nan. Her sister went to stay with her mother in another part of Germany. Both siblings grew up on the farm, so they were expected to pull their weight and lend a hand in the day to day running. The whole family literally worked hard to put food on the table.

I can't recall my mother ever saying, 'I love you'. I can only assume that my she didn't get a lot of affection from my Nan. My dad on the other hand, would hug us and everyone else he would meet. He also had a tough childhood growing up with six siblings in the countryside during the war. He was a generous man who would do anything for anyone if they asked him. For his own family he was hardly ever there. Despite everything that went on in the past, he is still my dad, even if I argue with him in my head sometimes. My relationship with my father has had its ups and downs throughout my life. This has made me who I am today, and I am grateful for having the parents I had as a child.

The Importance of Change

As I grew up, the time came for me to move out. In 1985 I moved into my friend's place. My friend and I worked in the same company and we got on perfectly from the first time we met. She is still my friend to this day and life has changed dramatically in all this time.

I remember that day in 1985. I was standing in the hallway talking to my brother quietly and he asked me if I was moving out. I told him that I was, and at that moment, my dad burst into the hallway. He told us off for whispering and demanded to know what was going on. When he found out I was leaving, he blew a fuse. I left and did not return after that. I didn't talk to my dad for 2 weeks. He stopped at the place where I worked. While I was getting into my car, he approached me and told me if I wanted the furniture from my room, he would bring it to me. My impression of my father was that he actually does not like arguing but it is like an in-built mechanism he has learned. He always eventually comes around once he has calmed down. It has always been the case up until now.

In 1987 I went to England to get married. I lived there for 6 months before returning to Germany with the army. I challenged myself with new things while I was there. I had three jobs: working at the pub at the weekend, in an office during the week and doing odd cleaning jobs for a bit of extra cash.

By trade I am a dressmaker among other things. I even did a fashion show in the barracks where my husband worked in Germany. I had created all the garments for the fashion show at the corporal's ball.

The place where I lived in Germany was filled with just army families back then. It was great as everyone knew each other. Our block was great, too. I was the dressmaker and below me a woman who was a hairdresser. I made many different garments for men and woman. I enjoyed the feeling of community spirit.

In 1990, when my first child was born, I stopped the dressmaking for a while and asked my dad, who was setting up a new business with a partner, if I could help out in order to earn a little bit extra for things like a holiday. My dad agreed. My friend Heike who also had little kids in the next block to me, looked after my six-month-old daughter, when I was at work. I knew she was in good hands.

The day came and I went down to the building site, not quite sure what I was to do. I did point brickwork and a man there showed me how to mix cement and sand, which I had to take up the scaffold to work with. It did take me a while, but I learned how to do it and I liked being outside.

My husband did not know what I was doing as he was away with the army. He was not exactly over the moon when he heard about me working on site, but eventually he seemed to be ok about it. The time came to be transferred and the army wanted my husband to move to Aberdeen, but we decided to stay in Germany.

My husband left the army and we moved into the upstairs of my parent's place. In 1980 my dad built a house on the same plot where the converted barn used to be. It was big enough for two families and had a main entrance and a hallway to separate the downstairs from the upstairs. Essentially, I had come back to the place I had run away from previously. Now it makes sense to me why and you will see.

I continued working every second week on the building site. As my mum was working shifts, she looked after my daughter a few hours every second week. The day came when the second child was on the way. I was out and about on the site, up and down the scaffold until four weeks prior to giving birth to my son. Being in the countryside and having all that space for the kids was great.

There were animals running around the yard and fresh fruit and vegetables in the garden.

In 1991, after my son was born, I continued working on the building site. My mum and a school friend, Elaine, looked after my kids every other week. My then husband was working in a bookbinder factory in town doing the early shift. He was not happy because he and my dad did not get on that well. Neither would talk to each other so they communicated through me. Here I was piggy-in-the-middle again.

It wasn't very long before it all fell apart. We argued a lot as communication was not my husband's strongest point. He did not say he was unhappy or that he would have loved to have returned to the UK. The influence from all sides for me was overwhelming and at that stage. I didn't listen to my inner self. The inevitable came and we got divorced.

When I was getting divorced, I had a friend working with me on the building site. Her husband had just thrown her out, so she stayed with me for a week until things settled down. My dad didn't approve and as always, made no bones about it. This was too much for me because I was in the middle of getting divorced and had my own proceedings going on with upcoming court. It didn't help being told by my dad that people in town had started talking about me and for that reason the authorities were going to take the kids away.

When I had a confrontation with my dad, it could take me up to two years to say what I needed to say, and when I did, it was an explosion inside of me. My energy was then gone for the rest of that day as everything would come up.

I corrected him on the spot, telling him they are my children, not his, and no one was going to take them away from me. The heartache my children felt was enough without him telling me what to do. I hated all the arguing. The divorce came and went in 1995. However, it was still a long road for us all to grow and heal.

The day I got my first awakening was when my kids were about four and five. It was the moment when I realised that I was doing the same as my parents did. I was repeating the process in bringing up my kids the way I grew up. The moment I realized I was saying the same things and doing the same negative things I experienced as a child was when I decided things had to change.

As the kids grew, we had one rule, which was no matter what is going on, we would talk about it and never hide emotions. This lesson I had learned from my relationship with my dad. We would be there for each other and support each other in every way.

While I was working in a male dominated environment in the building industry, I became the counsellor for everyone: builders, carpenters, tillers, plumbers, roofers, plasterers, owners etc. –

they confided in me as I was easy to talk to. The amount of life stories I have heard is astounding.

As time passed, I got together with an old classmate from school who was also working on the building site. Little did I know that I was going to be a personal therapist for years to come! Every day while we were working, we would talk about the challenges he had in his life. Back in school no one paid attention when he did not turn up. He went missing a lot back then. He had everything from depression to self-doubt, and a fear of heights and relationship issues too. He did not seem to have the happy hormone that is produced in your brain. He was on very strong anti-depressants, otherwise he could not even get up and go to work let alone talk to anyone. We worked together for 8 years and it took me a few years to get him to see a psychiatrist or counsellor or someone to help him more in depth.

When he did, he told me he knew all what this therapist was telling him. It was nothing new as he had informed himself via the internet. Well, it was worth a try. We continued to talk about the same things in different ways for 5 years or more every day. I am patient and a good listener but sometimes it got to me, and he knew it. Some days he would say we would not talk about his issues today because he could see I was not in the mood and he would tell me so. He was a very nice guy, but it was not possible for him to jump over his own shadow because he was trapped by the condition he perceived himself to be in.

He read a lot about the issues that concerned him, especially when it came to manhood. He believed what was written by so-called experts. The last time that I saw him was a Thursday evening in 2005. We had coffee together after work as usual. Everything was quite normal.

The next morning at around 11 a.m. his mum called me to tell me he was dead. I was shocked. He had started work on the building site as usual that Friday morning. Someone saw him falling to the ground. The ambulance was called, and his dad and paramedics went down to the building site. After several attempts to revive him, he was pronounced dead. He had always told me he did not want to grow old. At 40 years young, his wish was fulfilled.

In 2005 I had been working for UPS for four years in the preload department from 4.30am to 9 am. After that I went on the building site until the late afternoon. At the same time, I was creating my dressmaking studio. Not only that, I was busy doing Sunday markets too. 2005 was a very busy time for me.

I worked a lot. Most weekends, especially in the summer, the house was full of my kids and their friends. Many of the kids could not talk to their parents openly. So instead, they came to our house because my kids had always brought them home with them. Communication is so important no matter what trouble you're in. I was never really able to talk to my dad because I had learned a respect that I think was more based on fear. Just one look from him and I knew not to even bother saying anything. So, for that reason, I felt the need to be a listening ear for my children's friends.

Helping was always something I loved to do. Also being close to my kids was the most important thing. It was all about trusting and communicating and being there for both my children when they needed to talk. My kids were the most important thing and they still are. I am not a perfect parent, that is for sure, but had I continued to do the same as my parents, I would not have grown to where I am now.

2005 was also full of changes. I closed all my businesses and started to go back to school to change my career. I started to work in my friend's shop. The idea was to take over the shop eventually after I had finished my course. But everything changed.

My friend's wife and I decided to go to Ireland for 4 days because it was my last free weekend before starting afresh. Everyone who had been there always said it is so beautiful. On the evening before we went back, we were out in town and we met a few people, two brothers, to be exact, in Fitzsimons bar in Dublin. We started a conversation, which lasted half the night.

My friend went back to the B&B and I stayed on because we were laughing and enjoying each other's company so much.

Pat, one of the brothers, offered to give us both a lift to the airport the next day and we agreed. When he arrived and took us to the airport my friend remarked: "I'll give you 6 weeks and you'll be back in Ireland". I laughed then, but she was right.

At that time, it made no sense to me because I knew I had my life in Germany, and Pat had his life in Ireland. We returned to Germany, but Pat called me a couple of days later. The rest is history. We moved to Dublin at the end of October 2005. I remember it like it was yesterday; we arrived, and Pat picked us up. I said out loud, 'Finally I am home, I have arrived.'

Starting Over

Things changed a lot then in 2005, even for my kids. They finished their schooling in Ireland and I began to make new choices. I was always fascinated by energy. I did a lot of research because the human mind wants to know how things work. I learned more about personal development and I trained as an advanced practitioner in Neuro-Linguistic-Programming, hypnotherapy, psychotherapy and Reiki master. In Navan I started offering therapy in 2007 where I had many clients visit my practice. I have also facilitated courses, events and workshops in and around Navan related to my area of expertise.

When you learn to listen to your inner voice, there is an inner teacher that is so much greater than what you could imagine. Despite everything, the relationship with Pat did not work out as I had thought. However, I am sure now that it was for a reason. You can call it destiny. I don't really know. But one thing was certain; my inner voice was telling me that it was time to move on. At that time, my kids were living their own lives. For me, it was time to live my life, too.

Little did I know then what the universe had in store for me. I have always had a knowing that there is something greater than me and now I have been shown. Throughout this process, I learned that it is okay to start over; how important it is to never give up on yourself, no matter what.

In 2012 I went to India for the first time. It was a whole new level of personal growth at that point; not just for me but for all that are directly attached to me. When I went, I hadn't called my parents for three weeks. My mum knew where I was, but she hadn't told my dad. So, on my birthday while in India, I called my parents. I asked my mum to pass me on to my dad.

Firstly, she refused so I told her I wasn't going to tell my dad where I was, and it would be ok. So, when I spoke to my dad, I had found my inner calm place. It felt like talking to a totally different person. My dad was very calm. He didn't ask me where I was or why I hadn't rung. This was strange because if I hadn't called at least once a week like I was supposed to, he would give me the third degree. This time, he didn't. The shift in consciousness I had made also caused people in my life to shift, too. This is one example of that.

I have been safe all my life. I know that I have been guided, too. I always had strength when I needed it most. I was always protected from harm. Life is such a great teacher if you believe in yourself and if you trust beyond yourself because there is something far greater in all of us that cannot be put into words.

I told my mum that I love her on the phone for the first time 10 years ago. When I did this, my heart was racing as we had never said this to each other ever. My mum went silent and after a long minute she replied, "me too". I had tears rolling down my face and from then on when we spoke my mum waited to hear those words. My mum and I had spent many afternoons together when I was in Germany before coming to Ireland. Those three words were never said. I am so grateful that she was always there looking after the kids when I went to work. The relationship between me and my mum was completely healed a few years before 23rd July 2018 when she passed on. This was the most beautiful thing for me and my mum too because we did not need words. Sometimes we just knew by looking at each other.

When I tell my dad that I love him, he simply replies by saying he can't see that. I explained to my dad that love is not what you can see, only what you feel within your heart. I had explained this to him, but he is the way he is. I know he loves me in his own way. Learning to love yourself the way you are is the most beautiful thing because you shine and radiate that from the inside out. Love is unconditional.

The importance of the Present

In 2012 my mum was diagnosed with dementia. I went to Germany as much as I could. My daughter told me, 'You are not moving back to Germany because you will not be happy there.' That was true, very true. My daughter moved back to Germany to help out at the beginning of my mum's dementia. Returning to Germany was hard for her because living with my dad did not work out. So, she came back to Ireland eight months later.

My dad was not able to handle my mum forgetting things. In between those moments when she forgot, my mum would chew him up verbally and spit him out again. I had never seen my mum do that before. My mum was always a quiet woman who just worked a lot. We all did. That is something we learned from very early on. My mum did not like arguing because she had also carried a lot of pain from the past. Still, such feelings would rise to the surface. Then she would lash out with all the pent-up anger from all those years. This caused my dad to seek professional help in order to cope with the situation. This was something that he never would have done if my daughter had not gone back to Ireland.

Communication is so important not just with your family but also the communication that happens within you. I have been in beautiful relationships but the best one I encountered was with myself. Learning to connect with yourself helps you. You should trust the person that you are because there is only you inside. This was something I had to relearn.

To love unconditionally is beautiful because it frees you. It frees you from not having to control everything all of the time. It frees you from judging and wanting to be right. I love my kids and now grandchild. I can honestly say that even if I don't see them that much the connection is there. My kids are both married now, and I love to see them living their lives.

A meaningful life

In India I learned how to meditate. I experienced many different things, going into many deep processes of connecting with myself, my higher purpose and healing the past. It is like pealing an onion, layer by layer. You feel it, see it, hear it and sense it. Being in India allowed me to experience the spiritual side of life at a much more profound level then all the tools I had acquired before then. By connecting to the deeper part of myself, I developed meaning at a deeper level.

I have learned that the universe has many things in store for me. New things unfold every day. I have always had a knowing that there is something greater than me and once I learned to connect with myself, I learned to connect with my higher purpose.

Fast forwarding to now, my heart is calling to make a change in this world. For sure I feel an internal pulling. I know this because I have been shown what to do. That is why I am here. Connecting to the deeper part of myself allows me to say things that I wouldn't normally think of saying and to complete strangers as well. It is an inner "knowing" that seems to come from nowhere.

I have been asked how I do it. The only explanation I can give is that it is like the energy which runs from the switch to the light bulb in order to make it shine. It is also something you cannot see but you know it is there. The energy runs through the wires like it runs through you.

Some may think it is weird working with energy and healing and being connected to something that you cannot see. But by stilling the mind, it helps you to connect with your heart. You will be amazed what that can achieve. The heart is in actual fact, the strongest magnetic field in your body. So, it has far more power than the mind.

Passing on the change and message to others

Love is inside of you. Don't wait for someone to show you. The relationship you have within you is the most important one. The life journey you are on is full of emotions. It is energy in motion. You never stand still. You always move. Your intuition is what you were born with. Most of us lost it along the way in this busy world of competition. We are all programmed from birth with certain limitations and behavioural conditioning which can be broken through.

Love is what connects you internally. Your parents will always be there no matter where you are in the world. The moment you realise you are letting go of the past, you become aware there is only you inside your body and no one else, and you become lighter and feel brighter too. Life starts to flow easier when you act from your heart and not just your head.

Thoughts and emotions can eat you up inside without you even realising it. Stress and anguish take its toll on your body, causing all manner of ailments which can be traced back to your thoughts and feelings. It is not what you eat but what it is that is eating you. A good example would be someone suffering from stomach ulcers who tries everything to avoid certain foods which will aggravate the condition. In actual fact, the 'condition' is a symptom of the psyche which is crying out to be healed.

In this modern world we are taught to feel bad about ourselves. Makeover TV shows which are very popular, are all designed to make you feel unhappy with yourself because you don't fit the "perfect" format. You should embrace all that you are, perfect in every sense of life, from the moment you get up to the moment you go to sleep.

Life was given to you not to beat yourself up, but to see the beauty that you are. Live from the heart and make your mind your friend because your mind is not your enemy. There is a saying "You should learn to ride the donkey instead of letting the donkey ride you". If you can do that, then you are there. Befriend your mind as it is part of the beautiful you.

Trust that there is something far greater inside of you. Life has shown me that nothing is impossible once you let go of what does not serve you. I have learned to make necessary changes in my life in order to grow. Now I step aside and let my "higher self" come in and be the guide. This is far greater than intuition for me. This is the most amazing and beautiful gift that has been given to me and my heart is calling to do much greater things.

With each meditation and deep healing session I have facilitated over the past 7 years, I have come closer to my goal of realisation. Everything I have ever learned is now ready to fully shine because I know I have the ability to go much deeper within and help those that are seeking healing on different levels in life. I help people to reconnect and cut the ties of the past using the power of the sea to heal.

Here is a little guide of what I help you do while standing in the sea: I ask you to close your eyes, breath and focus on the sounds of the waves and feel the sand below your feet. As you feel the warmth from mother earth rising through your body, reconnecting you with your core. Experiencing all the sensations of safety at a much deeper level while I am standing beside you making sure your balance is perfect in order to let go of what does not serve you or hinders you from moving forward in life. The healing process goes far deeper for every individual then I could possibly explain in this short chapter.

Everything starts with little steps. You were not born and were able to walk and talk on the first day. It took a while. All the lessons in life that you have been given are teachers even challenges. When you start to become aware, you can see what is happening even inside of you.

This simple breathing exercise or a short-guided relaxation can help you to unwind and reconnect internally. Firstly, you can start by just sitting on your bed at night. Close your eyes, breathe in and out while saying "inhale, exhale.". After a while, you will find your mind becoming calmer. This is a great exercise before going to bed if you are having trouble silencing the brain chatter which is keeping you awake at night.

Letting go of the past is an important part of releasing stuck emotions inside of you that hold you back. It is a part of you being the change in your life. Never give up on yourself and trust you are here for a reason. You are not just a random number that showed up. You should be ready to move on to places you have never been to and do things that you never dared to do. Your life is a journey from the moment you arrive to the day you depart. Cherish it. Connect to it. Intuition is in all of us. It's time to tap back into your inner guide. The best temple is inside your heart. I found mine. Do you want to find yours too?

My journey brought me to Ireland and with it a deeper connection and spirituality. It has given me all the wonderful experiences which have allowed me to grow and develop. I love what I do and seeing others grow and develop hundreds of times is fascinating, amazing and so much more.

I have had the unique opportunity of helping people from all walks of life. I have been blessed with being able to go to India and to connect with people the world over. I am grateful for all the changes that have happened so far. I am ready to move to where I have not been and do things I did not dare to do because I am the change.

A Final Note

by Donna Kennedy

At the beginning of this book I told you that the only way to improve your life is to move out of your old frame of knowledge into a space where possibilities can unfold. Now, having read this book, I am delighted to say that the growth process has been activated. Whether you realise it or not, the stories, perspectives, ideas and suggestions within this book have altered your frame of knowledge and by default your energy and its vibration. In other words, the "on-switch" has been pressed. The question is, will you allow it to stay on or will you recoil back into your comfort zone? Only you can make that decision.

Years ago, the idea of changing and moving out of my old ways of thinking and behaving petrified me. Even though I wanted a better life, and I knew changing my ways would ultimately mean a better life for me and everyone around me, the familiar felt oddly more comfortable. Ironically, it felt safe! I didn't like feeling bad or stuck, but it was less daunting than embracing something new, something I wasn't familiar with and that I may not have full control over. However, I realised that we don't actually have control over anything in life. I had been fooling myself. The only thing we can control is how we *represent our experiences* of the world in our minds and the vibration we create around them. We can't control anything else.

It can take courage to embrace something new, but don't wait! I always had this put-it-off notion that someday I would *get* self-belief and confidence and then I would be ready to make changes. The truth is, nobody is ever ready, and self-belief or confidence are not things you can get or have anyway. They are states of being that come about from doing something often enough and knowing it worked out. And courage is not the absence of fear, it is simply realising that there is something more important than fear and giving yourself the permission to do it anyway, even if you're afraid. Feeling afraid of the unfamiliar is a normal part of life; *everyone* feels it. But if you're waiting for fear to go before you decide to become truly empowered, good luck to you! Fear is a feeling (an energetic shift) in response to how you are representing something in your mind. It is a generated state, not a concrete thing that can hurt you, even if it feels that way. If you change your thoughts (your representations), the feelings change with them. The feeling of fear turns into curiosity, then wonder, then excitement — just like when you were a kid.

The only difference between being an adult and being a kid is how much negative energy we attach to things. I only felt afraid of change because I created (unintentionally) a fearful mental representation of my experience of the world. I rehashed the past in fear, and I envisioned future scenarios in fear, over and over, adding more negative energy each time. If I had been told that re-representing my experiences (and their energy) in my mind would be so effective, I would have changed my life much more quickly and more easily. Do you need to change how you represent experiences in your mind and the level of energy you give to them?

When you have finished reading this book, I want you to close your eyes and visualise *your* best-self. Make it detailed and add good energy to it. If a negative thought pops into your mind, simply acknowledge it for what it is, but then let the wave pass. Give it permission to move along and dissipate. Negative energy has no place in your life anymore. It doesn't serve your higher purpose. Think good thoughts only.

Think of it as the first chapter of your new life. The world is open for your exploration, possibilities are endless, and you have so much potential to realise. You deserve the best! Power up and shine bright! You are not on your own, you have us, and *WE* Summit *Together*.

About the Authors

Donna Kennedy

Donna Kennedy is a highly sought-after mentor and professional speaker. She is a qualified psychologist and five times bestselling author. She founded the Women's Empowerment Summit and regularly features in media as an expert in the areas of personal development. Her work has been endorsed by many well-known personal development leaders, including Bob Proctor (The Secret), Brian Tracy (Goals/ Eat That Frog), Mark Victor Hansen (Chicken Soup for The Soul/The Power of Focus), Pat Slattery (Entrepreneur), Google and Boston Scientific, to name but a few.

She established her first business at age 23 and turned over €1 million in the first year. Her work has been used and referenced by several leading organisations, multi-nationals and banks to train staff and market product. Her academic work has also been recognised and published internationally by various faculties, including The American Journal of Psychology and The Irish Psychological Record.

However, at one point in her life she was afraid to cross the road on her own. She had several difficult challenges to overcome in the first half of her life but, having overcome them, she has proven that no matter what your circumstance, with the right approach and right strategies anything is possible!

"Listen to this girl, she knows what she is talking about!" - Bob Proctor (teacher in the book/movie, The Secret

"You are going to thank me in your prayers for recommending her to you." -Mark Victor Hansen (Chicken Soup for The Soul book series)

"I have been privileged to speak with Donna Kennedy. - Brian Tracy (Eat That Frog)

"Donna's talk in Google was extremely well received. We had a great turn out and found her content to be very strong!" - Google, European Head office

Contact Donna at www.donnakennedy.com

Kiera Ricci

Kiera Ricci is the director of an award-winning company, Bellisimos Academy. She operates a successful clinic, Bellisimos Aesthetics, and is an investor in Bellisimos Hair. She is qualified in TCM and Integrative Medicine and is a highly accomplished Aesthetics Practitioner.

She has been successful in establishing competent students resulting in professional and very rewarding careers has w, and has worked internationally, growing her brand to help her students on a global scale to champion and thrive in their professions. When delivering information to her students Kiera always keeps in mind the famous Bob Proctor quote, "You do not understand something, until you can explain it to someone else, and they understand it."

A true professional, Kiera is recognized for her clinical specialties throughout many countries, reaching Dubai, India and America, to name a few. She has always been entrepreneurial and from a young age has sought ways to analyse measurable results to achieve a productive outcome. Future planning is always at the forefront and continual self-development is key to her continuity in business and personal growth. Future plans are in line with prosperous expansion strategies, and all will be revealed in the near future. The futurity includes new methods and an advanced approach in business and entrepreneurship, taking a new direction on what is current.

Contact Kiera:

www.kieraricci.com

www.bellisimosacademy.com

Dorota Zurek

Dorota Zurek is originally from Poland. She holds a master's degree in political science, and she is a qualified financial adviser and experienced business analyst. She is a full-time working mother of two boys. The eldest son, Christian, is an eleven years old non-verbal autistic boy who has a medical condition called pseudo obstruction of the intestines, which causes him to live on amino acids only as he cannot digest and absorb regular food. Dorota says that Christian is her "petrol" and motivation to help and empower others to live happy, regardless of life challenges.

Dorota is a bestselling author and a neurodiversity, autism and disability advocate. She is a public speaker and life coach. In her free time, she loves to play with her kids, draw or paint and study languages. She speaks five languages already, including English, Polish, French, Spanish and Portuguese!

Contact Dorota see www.specialneedsmum.ie

Email: dorota.zurek87@gmail.com

Monika Florczyk

Monika Florczyk moved to Ireland at the age of 19. She started working as a sales assistant not long after arriving. Working in retail opened several opportunities for her. Gaining experience in all aspects of the business, including people management, financial strategy and sales inside, she discovered her passion for coaching and development. Monika decided to educate herself and she successfully completed a Higher Diploma in Business, a certificate in Training Delivery and Evaluation, a Diploma in Executive and Life Coaching and an Advanced Diploma in Human Resources. She focuses on the positive aspects of her life. She moved from retail, to human resources and finally to her current role as recruitment consultant in Excel Recruitment, a leader of the recruitment industry. Monika had to overcome several challenges in her life. Her story proves that no matter where you are from, what age you are or what your social status there is always a way to overcome obstacles and move towards achieving your dreams. She has also been a guest speaker at an event. Monika lives by the rule – YOU ARE ENOUGH!

Contact Monika at monicaflorczyk1@gmail.com

Alma Greene

Alma Greene is mother to an amazing daughter and is an advocate of Pranic healing and Arhatic yoga. In her spare time, she rescues and rehomes cats and kittens.

She has worked as the owner of Amber Clinic for over 20 years (www.amber.ie) where she specialises in Food Allergy and intolerance testing. She also works as a business coach helping people who want to take their business to the next level. You'll feel fully supported growing your practice and many of Alma's clients have reported consistent earnings of 5K per month.

Alma is qualified as a Kinesiologist and Homeopath and is extremely passionate about helping people to achieve their optimum potential.

Contact Alma at alma@amber.ie

Karen Keenan

Karen Keenan is a certified nutritional therapist and holds diplomas in both health science and life coaching. She is a leader in Runtalkrun and founded *Keenwellbeing in 2018,* a wellness service that focuses on helping individuals and groups find balance in mind-and body, whilst being supported on their journey. Karen believes that everyone deserves to experience *"The magic of feeling good about yourself through encouragement and support*." Not only that, Karen makes gorgeous healthy dishes so make sure to check out her cookery videos on social media!

Contact Karen on social media or at kkeenan1111@gmail.com

Una McGoey

Una McGoey established *Anu Change* to help and support individuals and businesses to clarify and realise their personal and business ambitions. Una's focus is on helping organisations to understand what motivates their employees so they can fulfil their full potential Una helps leaders and potential leaders gain clarity and lead with confidence while deepening their understanding of themselves and how they impact their teams and the wider organization through Personality Profiling (DISC). Specialising in Leadership Development Una delivers ECR & ECR360 (Emotional Capital Report) working with organisations helping them to retain and manage talent and Leadership Development. Una's qualifications include: Postgraduate - Leading and Managing People (NFQ L9). Professional Diploma in Financial Advice (QFA), Professional Diploma in Finance Services (Professional Banker NFQ L8). Certified Trainer and Accredited Practitioner Coach (APC) International Authority for Professional Coaching & Mentoring.

In her free time Una enjoys travelling, going to concerts and can sometimes be seen on her local Golf course and Tennis Court!

Contact Una at una@anuchange.com
www.anuchange.com

Emma Hill

Emma Hill is the Director of 3 multi award-winning Bird of Prey companies in Wales. A Pharmacology graduate from Newcastle University, Emma started her career working as a Sales Representative for GlaxoSmithKline. After realising her strength lay in Business Development and Relationship Management, she became their youngest Healthcare Manager. After meeting her husband and moving to West Wales, Emma was responsible for the Business across all the Health Boards in South Wales. In 2013 she decided to apply these skills to develop her own business and teamed up with her husband to grow Pembrokeshire Falconry. Three years later they opened Wales' largest owl centre, The Secret Owl Garden and a year after The British Bird of Prey Centre in the National Botanic Garden of Wales. As the only centre in the UK dedicated to native species, the aim is to give everyone the opportunity to interact with, and learn about, the birds of prey that can be found here in the UK and in doing so inspire communities to ensure their longevity. Emma is a confident public speaker having presented at Countryfile Live and she has made numerous TV & radio appearances for both the BBC and ITV.

"No One Will Protect What They Don't Care About; And No One Will Care About What They Have Never Experienced" - David Attenborough.

Contact Emma at:

www.britishbirdofpreycentre.co.uk

www.secretowlgarden.co.uk

Shelly Maher

Shelly was born on the 14.02.1971 in Tullamore. She grew up and spent her youth in a boarding school in Tipperary. After quitting school, as a young teenager she moved to Cornwall. She spent most of the time with her sister and her family and joined the family business. At this time, she started to struggle with her life and made some wrong choices. In 1993 her life changed for the better as she became a mother. She started looking at life differently and decided to help other people with their problems.

She had the privilege of being trained by some of the most successful people in wellbeing and business development and certified in advanced Ho'oponopono and tapping solutions. She and her partner now have a business in Tenerife called Beyond Yachting. You can find it on Facebook @beyondyachting.net and under www.beyondyachting.net Shelly is also a published author and can be contacted on Facebook @theshellyeffect

Lisa Mooney

Lisa Mooney is an American-born Irish woman and a single mother to two wonderful adult children. After pursuing a career in office administration for over 30+ years, she later fell in love with dancing and became a World Champion Line Dancer, along with other national and international wins, with the UCWDC (United Country Western Dance Council). She went on teach and coach, qualifying as a *Teacher of Dancing* with the IDTA (International Dance Teachers Association, Great Britain) and as a *Dance Teacher* with the CWDC (Country Western Dance Council). More recently, Lisa achieved a FETAC Level 5 certificate in Community and Health Services, an ITEC certificate in Holistic Health & Massage, certified with ACE (American Council of Exercise) in *Group Exercise Leadership* and is now pursuing a TEFL (Teach English as Foreign Language) qualification.

In her competitive years, she was a freelance writer to the Irish and UK magazine publication Co*untry Music Plus & Linedancer*, covering social and competition events and interviews with fellow comrades. With her love of dance and fitness, Lisa founded *DanceFit Ireland* in 2006 and developed her own dance fitness format, *Latin in Line,* before specialising in Zumba® fitness classes as a certified Zumba® Fitness Instructor, while becoming official caregiver to her mother.

An avid adventurer, Lisa has helped raise funds for charities through such activities as skydiving, abseiling, sleep outs, trekking, mini marathons, cycles, fun runs, skinny dipping, for the likes of Aware, CARI Foundation, Cycle Against Suicide, Pieta House, Aoibheann's Pink Tie, Purple House Cancer Support, Peter McVerry Trust, Focus Ireland, DePaul Ireland and Alzheimer's Society.

She has a passion for photography, travelling, scenic walking and cycling, the full moon, picturesque sunrises and sunsets. Having enjoyed two Camino de Santiago journeys already, another is due to take place this year across the Pyrenees Mountains and plans to lead a group of her own someday!

Having overcome many challenging times in her life, understanding and learning from these events has been paramount for Lisa in moving forward and she wants to put more of these life lessons into a future full book of her own.
If you would like to get in touch with Lisa, she can be reached at: lisainline@hotmail.com

Breeda Hurley

Breeda Hurley is a Kerry businesswoman who started her highly successful cleaning business over thirty years ago, and it's still thriving today. She has been the recipient of numerous awards, including the Lifetime Achievement Award for women in business. Breeda's trajectory through business and life hasn't always been smooth, but she has never let challenges and obstacles halt her progress. Instead she has learned to use them to her advantage. Nowadays Breeda is a keynote speaker, business mentor, and life coach where she draws on her vast well of experience and wisdom to help others achieve their goals. She also wrote her autobiography, *Survive and Thrive the journey of a lifetime*.

Breeda can be contacted at www.breedahurley.com

Robyn Walters

At 28 years old, Robyn Walters is a successful business entrepreneur. Owner of her own recruitment company, *RWR Recruitment*; she has won multiple awards within the recruitment sector in the UK. Robyn graduated in 2012 with a degree in Sociology from the University of Manchester before spending a year travelling the southern hemisphere. On her return she decided to embark on a career in recruitment after Googling 'what careers make the most money the quickest?!' Little did she know this would be an industry she flourished in, thriving on the excitement it brings each day, placing people into their dream jobs. After finding success within national recruitment companies, she knew she could take this challenging industry by storm, and in 2018 she founded *RWR Recruitment* and never looked back. Like the majority of the candidates she speaks to day to day, her own career aspirations drove her to make a change and disrupt the marketplace. This had made her a national leader in Manufacturing, IT, Finance and Business Support Contact Centre recruitment. By truly adding value to the sector, improving the recruitment experience for clients and candidates with a more focused and dedicated offering, she has made her mark. Her recruitment expertise has assisted companies to save money and time when recruiting low skilled positions to Director level. As a business owner Robyn has overcome many obstacles, yet always remains head strong to reach her goals. She has experienced that success isn't a straight line and the failures will provide the greatest foundations of your future. Her success at RWR Recruitment has inspired her to encourage others to not give up on their dreams as the impossible is always possible!

For more information see www.rwrrecruitment.co.uk

Rayner Davies

Rayner Davies is a multi-award-winning entrepreneur, Welsh Businesswoman of the Year, Entrepreneur of The Year, and most recently Institute of Directors – Family Businessperson of the Year. She is the co-founder and Managing Director of the multi-award-winning commercial cleaning business, A&R Contract Cleaning, South Wales, UK. A&R Contract Cleaning is a husband and wife run business with a multimillion-pound yearly turnover and over 200 hardworking, dedicated members of staff.

Rayner left school at 16 with very few qualifications, pregnant and claiming state benefits. She made a promise to herself then, that one day she would make something of her life. 18 years on and a lot of time spent working hard, taking courses and self-developing, at the age of 34 she has achieved extraordinary results. She has two beautiful children and a supportive husband and is described as a woman with a huge heart and a ball of fiery, positive energy.

Rayner has faced many of life's challenges and battled with depression for 14 years. Now a qualified NLP practitioner

Rayner's mission is to help inspire people and get them to believe in themselves. She is a confident, inspirational speaker, with radio experience and has been interviewed for a National Business and Health radio channel.

To date Rayner has raised over £35k for various charities. She feels blessed for what she has managed to achieve and is passionate about giving back. Rayner has done some extreme challenges from trekking in Patagonia mountains, cycling 600k, completed London's Virgin's Marathon 2019, organised and hosted several events, all to raise money for Velindre Cancer Centre and Mind Mental Health.

Rayner is proof that there is no glass ceiling, you really can achieve all you desire.

Contact Rayner at:

www.arcs-cleaning.co.uk

rayner@arcs-cleaning.co.uk

Liz Hickey

Liz is a warm and colourful character with a wealth of life experience. She has been married to Philip since 1981 and is mum to three young adults. Her background is in interior design, humanitarian aid and personal styling. She has qualifications in several healing practices. Liz is an advocate for lifelong learning. She went to college at IADT Dunlaoghaire in her fifties and achieved a degree in Business & Entrepreneurship, followed by post-grad qualifications from Innovation Academies in UCD and TCD culminating in a master's degree in Digital Entrepreneurship and followed by continued online learning. In her spare time Liz loves to grow fabulous flowers in her garden, create beautiful indoor and outdoor spaces, arrange simple special occasions for family and friends and collect 'Lifedeisgn moments'. Liz recently launched her Lifedesign business, a for-profit social enterprise, with online and offline 1-1 sessions, courses and trainings to teach people to problem solve creatively and empower them to lead wonderful lives, despite their challenges.

www.lizhickeylifedesign.com
www.thelifedesigninstitute.com
www.lizhickey.ie
Instagram.com/lizhickeylifedesign

Katharina Ashlin

Katharina Ashlin is a qualified clinical hypno/psychotherapist. She is also an NLP master coach and trainer, Reiki master, healer, empath and meditation teacher. She has been trained at the ICHP in Cork under the guidance of Dr. Joe Keaney, an internationally well-known hypno/psychotherapist. Having worked with clients in private practice since 2007, she has given clients the tools to enhance their lives. This book project by Donna Kennedy has given her the long-awaited opportunity to share her experiences and knowledge so that other people can empower themselves to make the necessary changes for a better life. In her spare time, Katharina likes to walk in nature or on the beach and spend time with her kids and grandchild.

Contact Katharina at www.katharinaashlin.com

Email info.katharina@gmail.com

Photographer

Shelley Rodgers

Shelley Rodgers began her photography career in 2000, attaining a BA Honours degree, PGCE, PGCFHE & MFA from The University of Ulster. Shelley went on to become an associate lecturer with tenure in photography at Bangor South East Regional College for 15 years. By 2013 the demand for Shelley's skill with a camera skyrocketed, enabling her work to reach hundreds of thousands of people by making regular appearances on bill boards across Belfast City and on the front covers of all the top commercial magazines including *Ulster Tatler, Ulster Life, and Ulster Bride* to name a few. Her photos were used for approximately 24 front covers in the space of 4 years.

As Shelley's photography was peaking in the commercial mainstream, her best friend (also her mother) Margaret, decided to team together and create the 'Shelley Rodgers Photography' business. Building a large photography studio together the work was rolling in until Margaret was sadly diagnosed with cancer and passed away in a matter of months.

During this period of illness, Shelley cared for Margaret until her passing and as an artist there were other less documented avenues, abundant in talent yet slightly off the beaten commercial track that intrigued her. Confiding in her mother, it was agreed by both to live without regret, to be bold and take a chance; now was time for Shelley Rodgers to create her own magazine that documented and promoted this wealth of artistic creativity. Margaret Rodgers passed in 2013, Shelley researched and by 2015 published her own fashion & arts-based magazine, now successfully running for five years. Initially called *EQUAL*

Magazine it is now called *WORLD EQUAL* Magazine, and it is available online in digital format and hard copy. It has also become the blueprint that gave rise to her becoming an organiser for events such as the ground-breaking and pioneering Belfast, London, Newry & Edinburgh Alternative Fashion Weeks.

In five years, Shelley Rodgers published almost twenty of her own magazines, some up to 200 pages of pure creative content. Shelley attracted & documented artists and fashion designers, both local and abroad, with her camera and magazine. Some designers, musicians and models travelled to Ireland from as far as London, Dublin, Wales, Scotland, India & France to be part of her alternative fashion runways. The talent and power of Shelley Rodgers and her photography is the sole driving force behind a five-year multi layered artistic exploration that has opened many doors to incredible opportunities, discovery and promotion between and for hundreds of people, from designers to models, other photographers, makeup artists, hair dressers,

Jewellery makers, milliners, authors, poets, aspiring film makers, musicians & artists, business commercial and alternative, who all have received vast media coverage. All this gained Shelley's *WORLD EQUAL* Magazine and alternative fashion events repeat yearly with prime-time television, radio and mainstream newspaper coverage, such as *The Irish News* to *Daily Mirror*, *Belfast Telegraph*, *Sunday Life* and *Sunday World.*

Now in 2020 Shelley has gained amazing endorsement and respect from a former Commodores frontman Mr. Skyler Jett, an American singer songwriter and music producer who has a Grammy Award for performing on Celine Dion's *'My Heart Will Go On'* The soundtrack to Hollywood's Blockbuster movie *'The Titanic'*, which is still, the biggest movie theme song of all time! Skyler has worked with all the greats like Whitney Houston, Aretha Franklin, Stevie Wonder, Mariah Carey to name only a few.

Shelley's mother, Margaret, was her best friend and business partner before she passed away and around that time Shelley was quoted saying to her *"I am not a business-person, I just take photographs. I love to capture the art and sculpture in an image, recording moments and memories. I'm not a particularly verbose person. I prefer the images to speak for themselves"*. Shelley Rodgers has since evolved into an artistic business entrepreneur that has inspired, trail blazed, pioneered, broke boundaries, set new trends and high standards in both the artistic, alternative and commercial industries to great acclaim, earning her the respect and support of her peers.

For more information about

WE Summit Together and

The Women's Empowerment Summit events

see www.wesummit.ie

Printed in Poland
by Amazon Fulfillment
Poland Sp. z o.o., Wrocław

55756679R00197